User Interface Inspection Methods

User Interface Inspection Methods

A User-Centered Design Method

Chauncey Wilson

ELSEVIER

AMSTERDAM • BOSTON • HEIDELBERG • LONDON
NEW YORK • OXFORD • PARIS • SAN DIEGO
SAN FRANCISCO • SINGAPORE • SYDNEY • TOKYO
Morgan Kaufmann is an imprint of Elsevier

Acquiring Editor: Meg Dunkerley
Development Editor: Heather Scherer
Project Manager: Mohana Natarajan

Morgan Kaufmann is an imprint of Elsevier
225 Wyman Street, Waltham, MA 02451, USA

First published 2014

Notices
Knowledge and best practice in this field are constantly changing. As new research
and experience broaden our understanding, changes in research methods, professional
practices, or medical treatment may become necessary.

Practitioners and researchers must always rely on their own experience and knowledge
in evaluating and using any information, methods, compounds, or experiments described
herein. In using such information or methods they should be mindful of their own safety
and the safety of others, including parties for whom they have a professional
responsibility.

To the fullest extent of the law, neither the Publisher nor the authors, contributors,
or editors, assume any liability for any injury and/or damage to persons or property
as a matter of products liability, negligence or otherwise, or from any use or operation
of any methods, products, instructions, or ideas contained in the material herein.

British Library Cataloguing-in-Publication Data
A catalogue record for this book is available from the British Library

Library of Congress Cataloging-in-Publication Data
A catalog record for this book is available from the Library of Congress

ISBN: 978-0-12-410391-7

For information on all MK publications
visit our website at *www.mkp.com*

This book has been manufactured using Print On Demand technology. Each copy
is produced to order and is limited to black ink. The online version of this book
will show color figures where appropriate.

Working together
to grow libraries in
developing countries

www.elsevier.com • www.bookaid.org

CONTENTS

INSPECTIONS AND WALKTHROUGHS

Inspections and walkthroughs started as software engineering methods for improving the quality of requirements, documentation, and code (Fagan, 1976; Gilb & Graham, 1993). The inspection and walkthrough approaches used in software engineering were partially borrowed by usability practitioners in the late 1980s and early 1990s for use in evaluating software and hardware for usability problems (Cockton, Woolrych, Hornbæk, & Frøkjær, 2012). Walkthroughs and inspections in the user experience (UX) domain were often viewed as informal (or semiformal), relatively fast, practical, and flexible (Hartson & Pyla, 2012)—attributes that make them appropriate for today's agile design environments.

Sidebar: Levels of Inspections in Software Engineering

Software inspections have been used as an effective quality assurance (QA) technique since the late 1970s. The focus of the software inspection process is the defect-detection activity where evaluators locate software defects during requirements, design, and development (Shull, Rus, & Basili, 2000). Following are the various levels of software inspections (Laitenberger & Atkinson, 1999):

- **Ad hoc approach**: No specific guidance is given on how to inspect a product. This approach has its UX counterpart in the individual expert review (Chapter 2).
- **Heuristic approach**: The evaluator is given a short list of general guidelines to help identify defects. This is a precursor of the heuristic evaluation process (Chapter 1).
- **Checklist approach**: The evaluator is given a list of questions or issues to consider.
- **Scenario-based approach**: The evaluator is given scenarios and specific procedures for finding problems in the appropriate representation of the product (requirements document, code, user interface prototype, working product). Most of the methods in this book are at least partly scenario-based.

These software inspections levels have counterparts in UX design methods ranging from ad hoc expert reviews (Chapter 2) to formal usability inspections (Chapter 6).

In the early 1990s, the user interface (UI) inspection gained acceptance as a way for both novices and experts to evaluate products and services. The classic book, *Usability Inspection Methods* (Nielsen & Mack, 1994), summarized the state of UI inspection methods in the early 1990s and provided both procedures and supporting research. Hundreds, perhaps thousands of articles have appeared on different UX inspection methods and approaches. These numerous articles discuss the strengths and weaknesses of particular inspection methods and often compare them to usability testing (Cockton et al., 2012).

In this book, six inspection-walkthrough methods are covered beginning with heuristic evaluation and ending with the formal usability inspection method.

Chapter 1 focuses on heuristic evaluation, perhaps the best-known inspection method. Heuristic evaluation generally requires a small group of evaluators to review a product against a set of general principles (the heuristics). A set of heuristics might include items like these, among others (Nielsen, 1993):

- Prevent errors
- Be consistent
- Provide clearly marked exits
- Speak the user's language.

Heuristic evaluation was originally conceived as a simple tool for usability practitioners and other groups, such as software developers or QA engineers, with relatively little training in usability. Chapter 1 describes the heuristic evaluation method and as well as ideas from researchers, practitioners, and this author, on how to improve the effectiveness of heuristic evaluation.

Chapter 2 focuses on the individual expert review, where a lone UX practitioner is asked to conduct a usability evaluation of a prototype or working product. This is more of a personal chapter, based on this author's experience as a consultant and individual contributor in commercial environments over the past thirty years. Many UX practitioners are asked for their expert evaluation of a product, often on short notice with no budget for testing or inspections with multiple evaluators. Although an individual expert review is not the optimal method or approach for finding the majority of usability problems, it is a common approach for many in consulting and corporate environments. This chapter focuses on how practitioners can increase their effectiveness when working alone on a usability evaluation.

An individual expert review can incorporate components of think-aloud testing, heuristic evaluation, checklist reviews, perspective-based inspections, and other evaluation methods.

Chapter 3 describes the perspective-based UI inspection, which is based on the principle that taking on different perspectives will increase the likelihood of finding UX problems. For example, you might ask a set of evaluators to each adopt different perspectives for their individual reviews; one person might be a "consistency czar" who looks at visual, interaction, and cross-product consistency. Another person might take on the role of an "efficiency expert" who focuses on shortcuts, automation, and the number of steps required to accomplish a task. Yet another person might take on the perspective of a "readability expert" who looks for text that is too small, low contrast between text and background, and excess verbiage. The persona-based inspection is a type of perspective-based inspection where selected colleagues assume the perspectives of the personas in reviewing the product. Persona-based reviews support a better UX by focusing inspections on the needs, background, tasks, and pain points of the different personas.

Chapter 4 covers the cognitive walkthrough, an inspection method that focuses on ease of learning (often referred to as "learnability"). The original targets for this method were walk-up-and-use systems such as automated banking machines, postal metering systems in malls, or infor-mation kiosks in museums. In the twenty-five years that the method has been in use, there have been several attempts to simplify it for use outside academia (Grigoreanu & Mohanna, 2013; Spencer, 2000). This chapter describes the original method and variations meant to reduce the com-plexity for evaluators.

The first four methods in this book do not generally require actual or potential users of a product. Chapter 5 describes the pluralistic walk-through (Bias, 1994) where users are invited to provide feedback on a design while members of a product team listen, observe the users, and ask questions when appropriate. This method is a form of participatory evaluation that involves entire product teams who are schooled in how to interact with users (e.g., they are asked to let the users speak first).

The formal usability inspection (FAA, n.d.; Kahn & Prail, 1994), the last of the six methods, is based on the formal software code inspection, which involves strict rules about preparation, evaluation procedures, data collection, and fixes. It is described in Chapter 6 that the formal usability inspection was best described by Kahn and Prail (1994) in the groundbreaking book, *Usability Inspection Methods* (Nielsen & Mack, 1994). The chapter includes a description of the formal usability inspection method and a discussion of some enhancements from the software engineering and quality literature. Formal inspections might be most appropriate for complex applications or products where there are serious consequences for errors (e.g., air traffic control systems, building design and construction, hospital support systems).

WHICH METHOD SHOULD YOU USE?

The inspection and walkthrough methods described in this book are all designed to uncover usability and UX problems within a computing system. So, which method should you use? Each chapter describes the relative effort required to apply a method and also provides detailed strengths and weaknesses that help you avoid mistakes. Table i.1 provides a quick summary about when to use the methods highlighted in this book based on the following criteria:

- **Phase of product development**. Some methods are useful across the product development cycle, while others are most suitable for particular phases. In general, inspections and walkthroughs are quite adaptable and can be used at multiple stages of the development cycle.
- **Usability attributes**. Which usability attributes are the focus of this method? Some methods, such as the heuristic evaluation, target multiple usability attributes (e.g., consistency, efficiency, learnability), while others, such as the cognitive walkthrough, focus on a particular attribute, for example, learnability for new or transfer users.
- **Training**. Heuristic evaluation requires "light" training on a set of usability principles and the review procedure. The cognitive walkthrough and formal usability inspections require more training, especially for team members who are not UX professionals.
- **User requirement**. Most inspection methods do not require users (although all of the methods can involve users as reviewers). Members of the product team and invited colleagues generally form

Table i.1 Attributes Affecting Your Choice of Inspection/Walkthrough Method					
Method	Phase of Product Development	Usability Attributes	Training	Overall Costs	Requires Users?
Heuristic evaluation	Requirements Conceptual design Detailed design Implementation	Learnability Efficiency Consistency Errors Flexibility	Low	Low	No
Perspective-based UI inspection	Conceptual design Detailed design Implementation	Learnability Efficiency Consistency Errors	Low to medium	Low	No
Cognitive walkthrough	Conceptual Design Detailed Design Implementation	Learnability	Medium to high	Medium	No
Pluralistic walkthrough	Conceptual design Detailed design Implementation	Learnability Efficiency Consistency Errors Flexibility	Medium	Medium to high	Yes
Formal usability inspection	Requirements Conceptual design Detailed design Implementation	Learnability Efficiency Consistency Errors Flexibility	High	High	No

the inspection team. In contrast, the pluralistic walkthrough involves users who review and evaluate prototypes with the product team.

You can mix and match these methods and use hybrids that combine methods to provide deeper coverage. For example, you can provide personas to members of a heuristic evaluation team and ask them to review products, apps, or services, based on the heuristics and the perspective of a particular persona.

There are many articles about "how" to conduct these various inspections and walkthroughs, but many are academic in nature. This book attempts to provide a solid procedural underpinning with enough practical detail for novices to apply these methods for the first time as well as tips and tricks that will improve the quality of your problem finding whether you are new to the field or a seasoned practitioner. If you have suggestions or ideas, please send them to the author at chauncey.wilson@gmail.com.

Heuristic Evaluation

Alternate Names: Expert review, heuristic inspection, usability inspection, peer review, user interface inspection.

Related Methods: Cognitive walkthrough, expert review, formal usability inspection, perspective-based user interface inspection, pluralistic walkthrough.

OVERVIEW OF HEURISTIC EVALUATION

A heuristic evaluation is a type of user interface (UI) or usability inspection where an individual, or a team of individuals, evaluates a specification, prototype, or product against a brief list of succinct usability or user experience (UX) principles or areas of concern (Nielsen, 1993; Nielsen & Molich, 1990). The heuristic evaluation method is one of the most common methods in user-centered design (UCD) for identifying usability problems (Rosenbaum, Rohn, & Humburg, 2000), although in some cases, what people refer to as a heuristic evaluation might be better categorized as an expert review (Chapter 2) because heuristics were mixed with additional principles and personal beliefs and knowledge about usability.

A *heuristic* is a commonsense rule or a simplified principle. A list of heuristics is meant as an aid or mnemonic device for the evaluators. Table 1.1 is a list of heuristics from Nielsen (1994a) that you might give to your team of evaluators to remind them about potential problem areas.

There are several general approaches for conducting a heuristic evaluation:

- **Object-based**. In an object-based heuristic evaluation, evaluators are asked to examine particular UI objects for problems related to the heuristics. These objects can include mobile screens, hardware

Table 1.1 A Set of Heuristics from Nielsen (1994a)
Example List of Heuristics
1. Visibility of system status
2. Match between system and the real world
3. User control and freedom
4. Consistency and standards
5. Error prevention
6. Recognition rather than recall
7. Flexibility and efficiency of use
8. Aesthetic and minimalist design
9. Help users recognize, diagnose, and recover from errors
10. Help and documentation

control panels, web pages, windows, dialog boxes, menus, controls (e.g., radio buttons, push buttons, and text fields), error messages, and keyboard assignments.

- **Task-based**. In the task-based approach, evaluators are given heuristics and a set of tasks to work through and are asked to report on problems related to heuristics that occur as they perform or simulate the tasks.
- **An object–task hybrid**. A hybrid approach combines the object and task approaches. Evaluators first work through a set of tasks looking for issues related to heuristics and then evaluate designated UI objects against the same heuristics. The hybrid approach is similar to the heuristic walkthrough (Sears, 1997), which is described later in this book.

In task-based or hybrid approaches, the choice of tasks for the team of evaluators is critical. Questions to consider when choosing tasks include the following:

- **Is the task realistic?** Simplistic tasks might not reveal serious problems.
- **What is the frequency of the task?** The frequency of the task might determine whether something is a problem or not. Consider a complex program that you use once a year (e.g., US tax programs). A program intended to be used once a year might require high initial learning support, much feedback, and repeated success messages—all features intended to support the infrequent user. These same features might be considered problems for the daily user of the same program (e.g., a tax accountant or financial advisor) who was interested in efficiency and doesn't want constant, irritating feedback messages.

- **What are the consequences of the task**? Will an error during a task result in a minor or major loss of data? Will someone die if there is task failure? If you are working on medical monitoring systems, the consequences of missed problems could be disastrous.
- **Are the data used in the task realistic**? We often use simple samples of data for usability evaluations because it is convenient, but you might reveal more problems with "dirty data."
- **Are you using data at the right scale**? Some tasks are easy with limited data sets (e.g., 100 or 1000 items) but very hard when tens of thousands or millions of items are involved. It is convenient to use small samples for task-based evaluations, but those small samples of test data may hide significant problems.

Multiple evaluators are recommended for heuristic evaluations, because different people who evaluate the same UI often identify quite different problems (Hertzum, Jacobsen, & Molich, 2002; Molich & Dumas, 2008; Nielsen, 1993) and also vary considerably in their ratings of the severity of identical problems (Molich, 2011).

●●●————————————————————————————

The Evaluator Effect in Usability Evaluation

The common finding that people who evaluate the usability of the same product report different sets of problems is called the "evaluator effect" (Hertzum & Jacobsen, 2001; Jacobsen, Hertzum, & John, 1998a,b). The effect can be seen in both testing and inspection studies. There are many potential causes for this effect including different backgrounds, different levels of expertise, the quality of the instructions for conducting an evaluation, knowledge of heuristics, knowledge of the tasks and environment, knowledge of the user, and the sheer number of problems that a complex system (e.g., creation-oriented applications like PhotoShop and AutoCAD), with many ways to use features and complete tasks, can present to users (Akers, Jeffries, Simpson, & Winograd, 2012). Knowing that evaluators will find different problems, from the practical point of view, can be dealt with by:

- Using multiple evaluators with both UX and domain knowledge.
- Training evaluators on the method and materials used (checklists, heuristics, tasks, etc.). Providing examples of violations of heuristics and training on severity scales can improve the quality of inspections and walkthroughs.
- Providing realistic scenarios, background on the users, and their work or play environments.

- Providing a common form for reporting results and training people on how to report problems.
- Providing evaluators with the UX dimensions (e.g., learnability, memorability efficiency, error prevention, and aesthetics) that are most critical to users.
- Considering how something might be a problem to a novice and a delighter to an expert.

This book discusses the strengths and weaknesses of each approach and provides tips from academic and practical perspectives on how to make inspections and walkthroughs more effective.

During the heuristic evaluation, evaluators can write down problems as they work independently, or they can think aloud while a colleague takes notes about the problems encountered during the evaluation. The results of all the evaluations can then be aggregated into a composite list of usability problems or issues and often prioritized based on severity, predicted frequency of occurrence, or other important dimensions (Yehuda & McGinn, 2007).

The literature on heuristic evaluation suggests that sessions should last one to two hours, not including the time required for training the people who will be the evaluators. This is a conservative estimate. Depending on the complexity of the product and the scope of the reviews, heuristic evaluations by a dedicated team might take days, with some invited participants focusing on particular areas for a few hours. In addition, the amount of time required to aggregate the results can be considerable depending on the number of evaluators, the method for reporting the problems (especially the granularity of the problem), and the complexity of the product.

●●●

Setting the Scope of Inspections

If you are asked to conduct a heuristic inspection by member of a product team or a client, make sure that you clarify the scope of the inspection. Open-ended inspections with no clear review boundaries can consume considerable time. Be explicit about what pages, screens, features, and UI objects are the focus of the inspection.

Heuristic evaluation is a popular method and one that is taught in many graduate human–computer interaction (HCI) programs, but also one of the more controversial for several reasons:

- **In some environments, the politics of inspections can be more challenging than the politics of actual testing**. Inspection results may be perceived as "just opinions," even though the results of inspections are of similar quality to usability testing (Molich, 2013).
- **Heuristics are often very general, and evaluators may have different conceptions of what the heuristics mean**. One early heuristic (Nielsen, 1993) is just "Consistency and Standards," which is so broad as to be nearly useless. Consistency, for example, is a complex issue and a simple heuristic does not capture this complexity (Wilson, 2009).
- **Evaluators are asked to use a prescribed set of heuristics as a guide, but most evaluators also apply subjective judgment and other principles** as the basis for reporting problems that often make the heuristic evaluation more of an individual expert review (see Chapter 2).
- **Evaluators report problems at different levels of granularity**; sometimes evaluators report things at a categorical level ("error messages are cryptic and lacking helpful information") and sometimes at an atomic level (Error message 132 has cryptic text that says "sysadm overflow: tetricular overflow—file is about to be conjugated").
- **It is easy to catch surface issues**—the poor text in a message, misalignment of controls, and superfluous text—but it is much harder to capture larger workflow issues. Sometimes the problems found in heuristic evaluation are "surface problems"—misalignments, ugly icons, and labels that are not quite clear. Those can all affect the UX, but deeper, task-related problems might be more critical issues for users.
- **Heuristic evaluation is prone to "false positives," reported problems that are, in actual use, not problems**. False positive can emerge because of incomplete knowledge of how people will use a product, evaluators' underestimation of user skills and adaptability, lack of understanding of usability and design principles, and flawed judgments about how an alternative design might perform in a particular context (Gilbert & Woolrych, 2001).

These issues are discussed later in the chapter with some recommendations about how to deal with their related controversies and minimize their impact.

WHEN SHOULD YOU USE HEURISTIC EVALUATION?

The primary goal of a heuristic evaluation is to reveal as many usability or design problems as possible at a relatively low cost. Heuristic evaluation, after all, was designed to be a discount usability method (relative to testing in a usability laboratory). A secondary (though very important) goal of the heuristic evaluation is to train members of the product team to recognize potential usability problems so they can be eliminated earlier in the design process.

Heuristic evaluations are a good fit in the following situations:

- You have limited (or no) access to users.
- You have an appropriate mix of design and domain expertise among potential evaluators.
- You need to produce an extremely fast review and do not have time to recruit participants and set up a full-fledged laboratory study.
- Your evaluators are dispersed around the world—a common situation.
- You are looking for breadth in your review. While usability testing is generally considered the best approach for finding usability problems in a product, most usability testing is designed to cover only small portions of products and services. Heuristic evaluation can provide additional breadth and complement other assessment techniques.
- Your clients have come to trust your judgment and, for many issues, will accept your recommendations without requiring you to conduct user testing or other more expensive evaluation methods. Of course, this carries some significant risk if a trusted usability practitioner fails to catch some very serious problems that result in schedule slips and lost revenue, but the same thing could happen in a usability test that doesn't include tasks that expose severe problems.
- Your project lacks significant funding for usability testing.

Heuristic evaluations can be conducted at any phase of the development cycle after problem definition (Table 1.2) where there is some representation of the UI (UI specification, functional specification, detailed storyboards, paper prototypes, working prototypes, or working product). Heuristic evaluations can be conducted iteratively from requirements definition to implementation to find and filter out usability issues and minimize rework by development.

Table 1.2 Phases of Development When Heuristic Evaluations Are Useful				
	✓	✓	✓	✓
Problem Definition	Requirements	Conceptual Design	Detailed Design	Implementation

Table 1.3 Relative Effort and Resources Required for Heuristic Evaluation—More Colored Bars Mean More Resources				
Overall Effort Required	Time for Planning and Conducting	Skills and Experience	Supplies and Equipment	Time for Data Analysis
▮▮▯▯▯▯	▮▮▯▯▯▯	▮▯▯▯▯▯	▮▯▯▯▯▯	▮▯▯▯▯▯

Table 1.3 illustrates the relative effort required, on average, to develop and use heuristic evaluation. Many heuristic evaluations require only limited resources; however, if your evaluation is used for high-risk situations, the resources (e.g., more evaluators and development of custom heuristics) required may increase considerably.

STRENGTHS

Heuristic evaluation has the following strengths:

- **The heuristic evaluation method is simple to explain (although the word "heuristic" is not).** At its most basic, you hand people a list of heuristics with some explanation and examples, provide them with a representation of the UI to review and ask them to list usability problems using the heuristics as a guide.
- **Heuristic evaluation is relatively fast if your focus is on a reasonable scope of features.** Heuristic evaluation can provide useful data relatively quickly, without the expense or effort associated with recruiting users.
- **Heuristic evaluations are similar to software code inspections,** and this similarity may make heuristic evaluations easier for product teams to accept than other usability evaluation methods.
- **Heuristic evaluations require no special resources** such as a usability laboratory (although for early prototypes of the product, you may need to work with a "test system") and can be used across a wide variety of products at different stages of development.
- **Heuristic evaluations increase awareness of common usability problems and serve as a method for training the product team about what**

aspects of design can lead to usability problems. One hidden strength of heuristic evaluation and the other methods in this book is that over the course of a year, colleagues who are involved in the evaluations will start to recognize design issues very early and eliminate at least some categories of problems.

WEAKNESSES

Heuristic evaluation has the following weaknesses:

- **Different evaluators often find different problems for the same product**. This "evaluator effect" (Jacobsen et al., 1998a,b) has implications for deciding what changes should be made to a design. What do you do if five evaluators each come up with quite different sets of problems (Kotval, Coyle, Santos, Vaughn, & Iden, 2007)? One tip here is to have a group meeting of all the evaluators where you walk through the problems, one by one, and discuss their validity and severity. The group discussion can help to determine which problems are "real" and which are "false positives" and to develop a consensus on the relative severity of different problems. Group reviews can also yield additional (missing) problems through the group interaction.
- **The heuristic evaluation method is based on finding usability problems**, but there is debate about what constitutes a problem and whether heuristic reviews are good at finding "real problems" (see a discussion of this in the "Major Issues in the Use of the Heuristic Evaluation" section). A problem for a beginner might be perceived as a positive feature for an expert and vice versa.
- **Heuristic reviews may not scale well for complex interfaces such as architectural design tools or Adobe Photoshop (Slavkovic & Cross, 1999)**. In complex interfaces, a small number of evaluators may find only a small percentage of the problems in an interface and may miss some serious problems. If you are evaluating complex tools, you may need to use multiple methods and combine the results across those methods.
- **Evaluators may not be the actual users of the system**. To strengthen the results of a heuristic evaluation, it is useful to involve domain specialists or to conduct several interviews with actual users to understand more about how they use the product.

- **In some situations, the evaluators have a vested interest in the product, which might blind them to some problems.** It is often useful to involve one or two outsiders who do not have a direct vested interest in the product to serve on the evaluation team.
- **Evaluators may report problems at different levels of granularity.** For example, one evaluator may list a global problem of "bad error messages" while another evaluator lists separate problems for each error message encountered. The instructions and training for a heuristic review should discuss the appropriate level of granularity. The facilitator of a heuristic evaluation will invariably have to extract important high-level issues from sets of specific problems.
- **Lack of clear rules for assigning severity judgments may yield major differences**; one evaluator says "minor" problem while others say "moderate" or "serious" problems. This author has examples of heuristic evaluations where different reviewers listed the same observation as both a problem and a "positive design feature."
- **Heuristic evaluation depends strongly on the quality and experience of the evaluators.** The value of conducting a heuristic evaluation with five novices who have limited knowledge of the domain and users may be questionable. The results of heuristic evaluation can match those of usability testing when your evaluators have ten years or more of experience in the usability domain (Molich, 2013).
- **Heuristic evaluation does not address solutions to problems.** Solutions are generally recommended by the facilitator or arrived at by discussion with the product team.

●●●————————————————————————————

Tips on Providing Solutions with the Results of a Heuristic Evaluation

1. Examine your problem set for global problems and propose a solution that will work for many individual instances of the same global problem.
2. If you found a number of comments about the organization of controls and information on a page, window, or dialog box, consider sketching a few rough prototypes of an improved design. Drawing a few rough solution sketches (rather than a single solution) gives developers some choice and increases the likelihood that they will take your suggestions seriously.
3. Provide a brief rationale for your recommendations on how to solve the problems. For example, you might explain that providing

a shortcut will improve productivity because the user does this task many times a day.

4. Make sure that your proposed solutions are consistent among themselves. Check for common patterns in the product or service and if the problem occurs in multiple places, consider whether a single solution will work.

- **Heuristic evaluation may not reveal problems that involve complex interactions by multiple users (e.g., in a collaborative work environment).**

●●● ───

Evaluations of Complex System May Require More Evaluators and Multiple Sets of Heuristics

Jaferian, Hawkey, Sotirakopoulos, Velez-Rohas, and Beznosov (2011) conducted a study of a very complex and collaborative environment—IT security management (ITSM)—comparing the number and severity of problems found using Nielsen's (1994a) heuristics versus a specialized set of ITSM heuristics. The result was that the two groups (ITSM heuristics versus Nielsen heuristics) of evaluators found different types of problems. The evaluators using the ITSM heuristics found more severe problems than the Nielsen heuristics group. The authors suggested that for complex systems (1) more evaluators are necessary when systems are complex, collaborative, and run by people with different risk tolerance, and that (2) it would be worthwhile to use both the Nielsen and domain-focused heuristics.

- **Product team members may feel that the heuristic evaluation is like a performance appraisal of their design skills and be nervous about this.** It is critical to let people know that it's good to find problems and that the results won't be used in any way as a measure of individual performance or skill. One way to mitigate the impact of a list of problems on colleagues or clients is to provide key positive aspects of the evaluation. The issue of reporting positive findings is discussed later in this chapter.

WHAT RESOURCES DO YOU NEED TO CONDUCT A HEURISTIC EVALUATION?

This section provides a brief description of the basic resources needed to conduct a heuristic evaluation.

Personnel, Participants, and Training

You need a facilitator who coordinates the activities of the evaluation team. The facilitator prepares the materials, conducts training (on the heuristic evaluation process, the heuristics chosen for the evaluation, and the features to be reviewed), arranges a representation of the UI to be available, collects the evaluations, compiles and analyzes the results, organizes a group review if necessary, prepares a report, and develops a heuristic evaluation infrastructure to track the results and examine trends and patterns in the data.

Facilitators need to be trained in the following:

- How to integrate this method with other usability evaluation methods
- Who to choose for the evaluation team
- How to integrate the problems from multiple reviewers
- The strengths and weaknesses of the method
- Methods for determining how serious the problems are
- Managing the different perspectives that various evaluators bring to the table, especially when the evaluators are from different groups, each having their own interest in the design.

A heuristic evaluation generally requires a team ranging from two to ten people (Hwang & Salvendy, 2010) with a mixture of usability, product, domain, and work experience. The size of the team will vary depending on the levels of experience of the evaluator, the scope of the evaluation, and the complexity of the software, tasks, and environment. Heuristic evaluation teams can benefit from some reviewers who are outside the product team to spot problems that might go unnoticed by those who are experienced with the product.

Depending on the size of your evaluation team, you may need assistance in compiling and debugging the results (determining whether different narrative accounts of the problems are in fact the same problem or different problems). If your heuristic evaluation procedure calls for think-aloud sessions where the evaluator reviews the product and a note taker records the problems, you will need note takers (preferably with some usability and product experience so they provide accurate descriptions of problems and heuristics).

of heuristics for assistive robotics by reviewing literature on accessibility, social robotics, cognitive psychology, perceptual psychology, and motor interactions with robotics. Desurvire and Wiberg (2008) examined the HCI, social learning, and self-efficacy research literature to develop a set of game approachability principles (GAP) that could be used for heuristic evaluation of beginning levels of game design.

2. Evaluators are trained on heuristics and the heuristic evaluation process to assure mutual understanding.
3. Evaluators are required to evaluate explicit features and apply specific usability criteria to each feature (Yehuda & McGinn, 2007).
4. Evaluators meet as a group to discuss their individual lists and combine the problems into a single list with agreed-on severity levels.
5. Evaluators develop one or more solutions for each problem or problem category.
6. Evaluators determine the effectiveness of the heuristic evaluation by tracking what problems were fixed, what solutions were implemented (compared to those suggested in the report), how much effort was expended on the change, and if there are meta-problems that should be addressed.

The next section presents general procedures for a heuristic evaluation. You will need to adapt these procedures to your particular organizational environment, development process, staff, and resources.

Planning a Heuristic Evaluation Session

Heuristic evaluations are considered informal, and one of the oft-cited advantages of the method is that "it does not require advance planning" (Nielsen & Molich, 1990, p. 255). On very small projects where the usability practitioners are well integrated into the process, this assertion can be true. But in many product development environments, advanced and detailed planning (especially the first time) is required. Following are the basic planning steps:

1. **Choose a team of evaluators**. The best evaluators are those with both domain and usability experience (Desurvire, 1994; Nielsen, 1992). For example, if you were evaluating a new travel site, you might seek out professional usability practitioners with travel software experience. If the product is complex, and the evaluators do not have much familiarity with the product, consider having one or

more domain specialists work with the evaluation team. When you consider the size and staffing of your heuristic review team, consider the following issues:

- Heuristic evaluations should generally not depend on a single evaluator. An evaluation team of three to five people is reasonable based on some modeling data and a cost–benefit analysis; however, the actual size of an evaluation team will depend on the following:
  - The heuristic and domain skills of your evaluators (Karoulis & Pombortsis, 2004). Kirmani and Rajasekaran (2007) provide a preliminary approach for assessing heuristic evaluation skills by comparing evaluators on the number of problems they find and the severity of the problems.
  - The priority associated with the product.
  - The complexity of the interface.
  - Your organization's tolerance of risk.
  - The breadth and depth of features that you are expected to cover.
  - Whether the system is mission-critical for your customers.
  - Whether the system presents safety or health hazards.

  For very large and complex systems (which include many websites, customer relationship management (CRM) software, mission-critical, and other high-risk applications), you may very well need more than three to five evaluators.

- **How much effort will it take to compile the individual lists into an aggregate list and prepare a report for your client**? Pulling together the evaluations from a large team with different views of problems, severities, and heuristics can be a daunting task. A short training session and the use of common (and simple) forms for reporting problems that allow easy merging of results can reduce the compilation effort.

- **What is the best mix of evaluators**? Double experts (those who have both domain and usability or HCI expertise) should be on evaluation teams if possible (Kirmani & Rajasekaran, 2007; Stone, Jarrett, Woodroffe, & Minocha, 2005). If there are few or no double experts, then you need to try and include both usability experts and domain experts. Other candidates for the evaluation team include quality engineers, technical writers, technical support specialists, technical analysts, information architects, and training specialists. You should also include a few evaluators from different projects who can look at the product with fresh eyes to avoid the problem of "familiarity blindness." For products that will have broad consumer use, you might consider inviting some nonexperts as well as some edge users who might stretch the limits of the product and reveal usability problems that would otherwise go unnoticed. Cockton Woolrych, Hornbæk, and Frøkjær (2012) recommend that evaluation teams include people who have a good mix of the following distributed cognitive resources (DCRs) to find the widest range of problems:

- **User knowledge** (knowledge of user skills, abilities, training, and work environments)
- **Task knowledge** (detailed knowledge of the task and more importantly, how users perform in both individual and collective tasks)
- **Domain knowledge** (knowledge of the target domain—finance, engineering, games)
- **Design knowledge** (knowledge and experience with UI design, interaction design, and visual design)
- **Interaction knowledge** (how do people really work with a system, which might not be how product teams think they use the system)
- **Technical knowledge** (e.g., knowledge of browsers, cloud computing, and iOS)
- **Product knowledge** (specific knowledge of the target product, its features, and capabilities).

2. **Decide which heuristics are most useful for your evaluation**. Numerous sets of general heuristics are available. Table 1.4 provides four examples of different sets of heuristics.

The major issues around the choice of heuristics include the following:

- **Relevance**. Are the heuristics relevant to the domain and product? Some general heuristics like those in Table 1.4 are general enough to be relevant to many types of computing systems. However, if you are evaluating a call center application where extreme efficiency is a key attribute, you may need to include some domain-specific heuristics that are relevant to the call center environment and focus on high efficiency. As discussed earlier in this chapter, a combination of general heuristics and domain heuristics might be the best approach for more complex products and services.

Table 1.4 Examples of Sets of Heuristics

Nielsen Heuristics (Nielsen, 1994b)	Groupware Heuristics (Baker, Greenberg, & Gutwin, 2002)
1. Visibility of system status 2. Match between system and the real world 3. User control and freedom 4. Consistency and standards 5. Error prevention 6. Recognition rather than recall 7. Flexibility and efficiency of use 8. Aesthetic and minimalist design 9. Help users recognize, diagnose, and recover from errors 10. Help and documentation	1. Provide the means for intentional and appropriate verbal communication 2. Provide the means for intentional and appropriate gestural communication 3. Provide consequential communication of an individual's embodiment 4. Provide consequential communication of shared artifacts (i.e., artifact feedthrough) 5. Provide protection 6. Manage the transitions between tightly coupled and loosely coupled collaboration 7. Support people with the coordination of their actions 8. Facilitate finding collaborators and establishing contact
Research-Based Heuristics (Gerhardt-Powals, 1996)	General Heuristics (Weinschenk & Barker, 2000)
1. Automate unwanted workload 2. Reduce uncertainty 3. Fuse data 4. Present new information with meaningful aids to interpretation—use a familiar framework, making it easier to absorb 5. Use names that are conceptually related to function 6. Group data in consistently meaningful ways to decrease search time 7. Limit data-driven tasks 8. Include in the displays only that information needed by the user at a given time 9. Provide multiple coding of data when appropriate 10. Practice judicious redundancy (to resolve the possible conflict between heuristics 6 and 8)	1. User control 2. Human limitations 3. Modal integrity 4. Accommodation 5. Linguistic clarity 6. Aesthetic integrity 7. Simplicity 8. Predictability 9. Interpretation 10. Accuracy 11. Technical clarity 12. Flexibility 13. Fulfillment 14. Cultural propriety 15. Suitable tempo 16. Consistency 17. User support 18. Precision 19. Forgiveness 20. Responsiveness

- **Understandability**. Will the heuristics be understood by all members of the analysis team? One of the issues with the research-based guidelines (see Table 1.4) proposed by Gerhardt-Powals (1996) is that the evaluators have to be quite familiar with cognitive psychology and human factors research and principles to understand just what it means to "Limit data-driven tasks" and "fuse data." Even simple-sounding heuristics such as "chunking" can be misunderstood. There is also the issue of consistent understanding of the heuristics. Do you evaluators have a reasonably consistent understanding of heuristics such as "consistency" and "prevent errors"? There are many types of consistency and many types of error prevention. One way to improve understandability is to include subcategories under each heuristic such as:

Consistency
- Consistency with the way people work (Grudin, 1989; Wilson, 2009)
- Terminology/language consistency
- Visual consistency
- Interaction consistency
- Metaphorical consistency
- Layout consistency
- Consistency with other similar features in the existing product
- Error prevention consistency
- Consistency with operating system (OS) guidelines.

- **Use as memory aids**. Are the heuristics good memory aids for the many detailed guidelines they are meant to represent? For example, does the heuristic "error prevention" prompt the novice or expert to consider the hundreds of guidelines regarding good labeling, input format hints, the use of abbreviations, explicit constraints on the allowable range of values, and other techniques or principles for actually preventing errors?
- **Validity**. Is there proof that applying a particular set of heuristics will lead to better products? Bailey (1999) argues for the use of research-based heuristics where the literature shows that particular methods have an actual impact on performance.

3. **Develop an infrastructure for collecting, organizing, tracking, and reporting on the results of the heuristic evaluation.** The infrastructure can include the following:
   - Paper or online forms for collecting problems. These forms can include the following:
     - A brief description of the problem
     - Where the problem was found
     - The number of users who might experience the problem
     - The frequency/persistence of the problem for various classes of users
     - The severity of the problem
     - Whether the problem was local (found in only one place in the UI) or global (found in multiple places in the UI) (Dumas & Redish, pp. 322–323) (Table 1.5).

Table 1.5 Template for Collecting Problems in a Heuristic Evaluation					
Problem/Problem Location	Heuristic	Severity	Frequency/ Persistence	Extent (Local versus Global)	Rationale/ Notes

- A training package where you explain, for example, what heuristics such as "match between system and the real world" really mean.
- One or more report formats geared to the needs of your clients. The reports are used to communicate the results of the evaluation, suggest possible solutions, and provide metrics for teams and managers.
- A database or some method for aggregating, organizing, and tracking problems.
- A method for tracking what problems will be dealt with by development or another group (e.g., some problems may be the responsibility of the documentation team) and some measure of the actual number of problems from the evaluation that were fixed.
- An explicit description of how to assess the severity of usability problems. This description should include definitions of severity levels, examples of problems for each severity level, and a discussion of why they received a particular severity rating.

4. **Conduct a short training session with potential evaluators who have not been part of earlier evaluations**. This step is optional, but from this author's experience, it's an activity that will increase the quality of reviews within an organization. Training can cover the heuristic evaluation process, the heuristics that will be used, the severity scale (if applicable), the reporting form, and the level of detail expected when describing usability problems. If your evaluators are new to the method, consider conducting a practice heuristic evaluation and discussing the results.

5. **Provide the evaluators with some context to help them understand the business objectives, the personas or user profiles, the user goals and tasks, and the environments where the product will be used**. The amount of background that you provide might vary according to

complexity. If you are evaluating a walk-up-and-use interface such as a mall kiosk, you might simply tell your evaluators the purpose of the system and not much else. If your product is complex, such as a financial trading system or big data visualization tool, the evaluators will need additional details (Lauesen, 2005).

6. **Provide the team with an overview of the prototype or working system that they will be evaluating**. This overview includes the following:
   * How to get access to the system
   * What the product is used for
   * The major features
   * Any limitations that they need to know about
   * Whether anything the evaluator does could cause any damage to the product that is not recoverable
   * A description of the sample data and some background on how realistic those data are
   * Who to call for help (prototype systems can often be temperamental, and reliable support can save time and reduce frustration).

7. **Choose which approach to your heuristic evaluation is most appropriate given the state of the product**. The basic approaches are listed here:
   * Create a set of important task scenarios, and ask your evaluators to work through the scenarios, noting any problems that emerge.
   * Give your evaluators a set of goals, and ask them to use the product to achieve those goals. For example, if you were testing a working prototype of an e-commerce website, you might ask each person on the team to use the prototype "buy something that they need in the next month" and record problems as they try to make their purchases.
   * Ask the evaluators to review specific UI objects (pages in a website, windows and dialog boxes, menus, error messages) and record violations of heuristics.
   * Ask the evaluators to evaluate a product based on a combination of task scenarios, goals, and specific UI objects and then report problems that emerge from this combination of approaches. This is the most powerful approach, but it takes more planning and effort.

Conducting a Heuristic Evaluation
Follow these steps to conduct a heuristic evaluation:

1. **Orient the evaluators**. Provide the team with the materials required for the evaluation of the particular representation of the UI that is

available (a catalog of screen shots, a paper prototype, a set of wireframes with clickable links, a working prototype, or even a competitive product). Review the procedures with the entire group if possible, and field any questions that the evaluation team might have. Go over the schedule for the evaluation. Provide any passwords and access information that people didn't get in the training and overview session.

●●●——

Provide an Exemplary Sample of a Problem Report

A best practice for heuristic evaluation or any other usability evaluation method is to provide an exemplary problem report that provides some clues to new evaluators about what makes a "great problem report." This exemplar can provide examples of the amount of detail needed and what information is critical. For example, it is important in a completed problem reporting form to note exactly where the problem occurs—which screen, dialog, page, window, or application.

——

2. **Ask the evaluators to conduct individual evaluations of the UI.** Because the evaluations are generally done individually, there is no way to strictly control how each person goes about the review, but you might suggest a particular review sequence such as the following:
   a. Familiarize yourself with any background information (goals, personas, environment descriptions) on the product.
   b. Walk through the task scenarios.
   c. Review any additional parts of the product that were not part of the task scenarios.
   d. If you have questions about the review process, contact the leader of the evaluation. If you have technical or domain questions, contact the designated technical expert.
3. **Advise your evaluators to list problems separately, even if the same problem recurs in different places in the UI.** It is important to know if problems are pervasive (global) or isolated (local). If you find the same problem in many places (e.g., a bad search UI in different areas of a product or bad error messages that occur in editable data tables), then this might alert you to systemic problems that require an architectural change.
4. **If your heuristic evaluation will last over several days, consider reconvening your evaluation team at the end of the first day of review so that issues about the procedure or product can be discussed and**

ironed out before they have gone too far in the evaluation. If a group meeting isn't possible, you might contact your evaluators and ask if they have any questions or issues.

5. **Collect the heuristic evaluation forms containing the list of problems found by each evaluator**. Let the evaluators know that you may call them if you have any questions.

After the Heuristic Evaluations by Individuals

When the evaluations are complete, follow these steps:

1. **Compile the individual lists of problems into a single list, and then decide on how to arrive at the severity ratings**. There are several techniques for coming up with severity ratings. If your data collection form asked your evaluators to rate the perceived severity of problems, you could take an average of the scores for problems found by multiple evaluators. A better solution is to set up a meeting (face-to-face or remote) to review each problem and ask each evaluator to indicate how severe each problem is. If there is too much variability in severity scores for the same problem (e.g., you have three evaluators—one rates the problem as severe (5), another rates the problem as moderate (3), and yet another rates it as minor (1)), you can discuss the differences and arrive at a consensus rating. This type of discussion will lead to a better understanding of issues within your product purview and sharpen the skills of the evaluators.

2. **Organize the problems in a way that is useful to the product team**. For example, you can highlight the most serious problems in an executive summary and then organize individual problems by their location in the product. A useful activity before you conduct a heuristic evaluation is to show a sample report to the product team (especially the development manager) and get their feedback on the usefulness and usability of the report. Heuristic evaluation reports sometimes recommend potential solutions for the problems that emerged. Whether you make general or concrete recommendations sometimes depends on your role and the politics of your organization. If you have a design team, you may be pressured to explain the problem, but not suggest anything more than a very general solution because that is the design team's responsibility. They are the designers—you are the evaluator.

3. **Consider whether you want to have a group meeting of the evaluators, developers, and designers to prioritize the results and discuss recommended solutions to the problems.**
4. **Catalog, prioritize, and assign problems, themes, and issues to the appropriate members of the product team.** Arrange subsequent meetings to review potential solutions for the important problems.
5. **Validate the changes to the product with user tests, beta feedback, or other evaluation methods whenever possible.**

VARIATIONS AND EXTENSIONS OF THE HEURISTIC EVALUATION METHOD

This section describes variations and extensions of the heuristic evaluation method from the research and practitioner literature.

The Group Heuristic Evaluation with Minimal Preparation

With the widespread move to agile development, some UX and agile teams are doing group heuristic evaluations where a team of five to ten UX, domain, and product experts review a feature or set of features against a set of heuristics during a single group session. Generally, the product owner or the designer of a feature will walkthrough through common tasks and the evaluators will call out violations of heuristics. The problems are noted by recorder. Questions for clarification are allowed, but not discussion about design solutions. These group heuristic evaluations can last one to three hours (three hours is about the limit of concentration). Often, a second session with a core group is used to discuss factors (e.g., frequency, extent, impact) affecting the severity of the potential problems.

Crowdsourced Heuristic Evaluation

With current collaboration tools, it is possible to expand the scope of a heuristic evaluation to include dozens of participants. You can provide users and UX practitioners with prototypes online and ask them to describe problems, the severity of each problem, and the rationale (e.g., the heuristic) for each problem. At the time of this writing, there seems to be relatively little academic discussion of crowdsourced heuristic evaluation.

Participatory Heuristic Evaluation

Muller, Matheson, Page, and Gallup (1998, p. 14) extend the basic heuristic evaluation method by adding a new category of heuristics called "Task and Work Support." In addition, Muller included users (called "work-domain experts") in the evaluation and suggested that participatory heuristic evaluation (PHE) can be nearly as cost-effective as heuristic evaluation if users are close by and easy to recruit. Muller and his colleagues discuss how the earlier sets of heuristics were generally product oriented and concerned with problems in isolation. The task and work support heuristics focus on user goals (produce quality work, keep sensitive material private, enhance my skills) and a positive experience in the workplace.

●●●———————————————————————————————

Task and Work Support Heuristics (Muller et al., 1998)

Skills. The system supports, extends, supplements, or enhances the user's skills, background knowledge, and expertise. The system does not replace them. Wizards support, extend, or execute decisions made by users.

Pleasurable and respectful interaction with the user. The user's interactions with the system enhance the quality of her or his experience. The user is treated with respect. The design reflects the user's professional role, personal identity, or intention. The design is aesthetically pleasing—with an appropriate balance of artistic as well as functional value.

Quality work. The system supports the user in delivering quality work to her or his clients (if appropriate). Attributes of quality work include timeliness, accuracy, aesthetic appeal, and appropriate levels of completeness.

Privacy. The system helps the user to protect personal or private information—belonging to the user or to her or his clients.

Cooperative Evaluation

Monk, Wright, Haber, and Davenport (1993) published a procedural guide to a technique they called "cooperative evaluation." Cooperative evaluation involves pairing a user and designer in an evaluation of a working version of a product. In the cooperative evaluation, users can freely ask questions of the designer, and the designer can ask questions of the user. The method, like early versions of heuristic evaluation, is aimed at designers with limited human factors or UX backgrounds.

Heuristic Walkthrough

Sears (1997) developed a technique called a "heuristic walkthrough" that had some of the attributes of three UCD methods: (1) a heuristic evaluation, (2) a perspective-based inspection, and (3) a cognitive walk-through. In Sears's method, the evaluators were given a prioritized list of user tasks, a set of heuristics, and "thought-provoking questions" derived from the cognitive walkthrough method described in Chapter 3.

Sears divided the walkthrough into two phases. Phase 1 required evaluators to conduct a task-based review that involved working through the tasks and the thought-provoking questions for the tasks. Phase 2 involved free exploration of the UI and an evaluation against a list of usability heuristics. Sears found that this hybrid method yielded fewer false positives than a heuristic evaluation and more real problems than the cognitive walkthrough method. The primary difference between the heuristic walkthrough and the two-pass heuristic evaluation (where the inspectors use task scenarios in one pass and then do either guided or free exploration of the UI) is the inclusion of the thought-provoking questions.

HE-Plus Method

Chattratichart and Lindgaard (2008) describe a variation on the heuristic evaluation method called HE-Plus. HE-Plus uses the heuristics described by Nielsen (1993), but also adds a "usability problems profile" that lists common problem areas for the system being evaluated. Here is an example of a usability problem profile from the 2008 paper that shows eight problem areas for a hotel reservation site (Chattratichart & Lindgaard, 2008, p. 2216).

1. Information content
2. Navigation
3. Graphics and UI objects
4. System features, functionality, defaults, interaction with I/O devices
5. Formatting and layout
6. Wording and language
7. Feedback, help, and error messages
8. Pan-disability accessibility.

The authors provide some research support for the superiority of the HE-Plus method that combines both heuristics and a usability problem profile. The practitioner takeaway here is that the combination of heuristics and a list of common problem areas for the type of software you are focused on can improve the quality of your heuristic evaluation.

MAJOR ISSUES IN THE USE OF THE HEURISTIC EVALUATION METHOD

The heuristic evaluation method has seen much scrutiny since the early 1990s. Some of the major issues that will face practitioners are described in the section below.

How Does the UX Team Generate Heuristics When the Basic Set Is Not Sufficient?

While a detailed discussion about how to generate custom heuristics is beyond the scope of this book, a few brief notes might be helpful. There are several ways to generate heuristics when the basic sets are not sufficient. First and most efficient, you can search the literature for heuristics that have been used to evaluate the usability of products and services similar to yours. The ACM Digital Library (http://dl.acm.org) is an excellent source of heuristics dealing with a wide range of products and particular areas such as accessibility, security, game design, ambient displays, information architecture, and persuasive technologies. The ACM research literature often describes how new heuristics are generated and validated (usually by examining how well the new heuristics support the identification of known problems in related products and services).

A second approach (Mankoff, Dey, Hsieh, Kientz, Lederer, & Ames, 2003) is to develop a list of the primary goals of a system, see how well standard lists of heuristics meet the primary goals of a system, remove irrelevant heuristics, and modify relevant ones to focus on the goals of your target system. Brainstorm new heuristics with experts, and then have an additional group of designers and domain experts review and refine the heuristics using a workshop or survey method. After developing a new set of heuristics, you can test them against a known system to validate the efficacy.

Do Heuristic Evaluations Find "Real" Problems?

There is a major debate in the field about what constitutes a usability problem (Wilson, 2007). Bailey, Allan, and Raiello (1992) suggested that many of the "problems" found in heuristic evaluations were not actually performance or preference problems at all (they called these "false positives"). Other researchers have noted that heuristic evaluations miss many usability problems. Doubleday, Ryan, Springett, and Sutcliffe (1997) compared the problems found in a heuristic evaluation using five UCD experts with the problems that emerged from end-user testing.

Doubleday and her colleagues found that the heuristic evaluation found only fifteen of the thirty-eight problems (39%) that occurred during end-user testing. In comparison, the end users experienced only 40% of the problems predicted in the heuristic evaluation. Following are the possible reasons for these differences:

- Heuristic evaluators, even when working with task scenarios, are not immersed in the task in the same way as end users.
- Heuristic evaluators who are experts in areas such as Windows or web interaction styles may not experience some very basic problems that can lead to confused users. For example, elderly users, unlike most UCD experts, may have no idea that they should avoid clicking on advertising buttons that say "Click here to get rid of viruses." Elderly users who are new to computing and the web may think that they *must* click on those buttons. UCD experts might not be able to easily emulate the issues and problems experienced by particular populations (brand-new users, kids, multitasking users who are trying to talk on the phone, elderly users, physically/mentally challenged users).
- The granularity of the problems in the heuristic evaluations differed. Some evaluators specified very general problems such as "missing shortcuts," whereas others listed "there is no shortcut for the Browse feature."

The definition of "problem" used in these studies is often "something that was found in a usability test with actual users." Studies that examine the validity and reliability of heuristic evaluations often base the efficacy of heuristic evaluation on a comparison with the problem list derived from usability testing. However, user testing is not a foolproof method for generating the "true and complete" problem lists for anything beyond extremely simple UI objects. The results of usability testing are affected by facilitation experience, the particular tasks chosen, the choice of and background of participants, the size of the database, and other factors. Cockton et al. (2012) discuss many issues associated with the reliability and validity of usability inspection methods, including heuristic evaluations.

●●●————————————————————————————————

Triangulation of Problems

The most powerful method for determining what the "real" problems are is triangulation (Wilson, 2006), in which you use multiple methods (e.g., cognitive walkthroughs, heuristic evaluations, user testing, feedback from customers on prior versions of the product, reviews of technical support call records, and participatory design sessions) to find the problems with a product. Problems that are found repeatedly using different methods with different users on different systems are the real problems that should receive the highest priority in the development schedule.

Does Heuristic Evaluation Lead to Better Products?

Heuristic evaluations might be the most-used usability method (Rosenbaum et al., 2000), but the connection between finding problems and measurable improvements in products is difficult to establish. To establish this connection, you need to do the following:

- Find problems.
- Come up with a good solution for each problem.
- Persuade developers to implement the solution as you recommended.
- Test the final product taking into account that some fixes will introduce completely new problems.

How Much Does Expertise Matter?

One of the consistent findings of the research on various forms of usability evaluation methods is that expertise does matter. Three major types of expertise affect the results of heuristic evaluations: knowledge of the heuristic evaluation method and principles, knowledge of the domain, and knowledge of the expected context of use (Cockton et al., 2002, p. 1127). Lack of knowledge in these three areas can lead to increased false positives and missed problems. The following are methods of improving expertise:

- Conduct a training session with a focus on the set of heuristics that you are using and definitions of problems and severity levels.
- Sponsor some seminars on design topics to prime potential evaluators if you are working in a corporate environment.
- Use domain-specific heuristics, which can be developed from usability testing or competitive analysis and can be used to improve the thoroughness of heuristic evaluations. The drawback with domain-specific heuristics is that it takes time and domain expertise to develop and validate them.

- Provide some context-of-use information for the team. For example, you might discuss common scenarios, user profiles, and background information on the main issues for this type of product.
- Invite domain experts to be part of your review team and, if possible, have double experts who have both usability and domain knowledge.

Should Inspections and Walkthroughs Highlight Positive Aspects of a Product's UI?

Inspections and walkthroughs are heavily focused on problems and seldom highlight positive aspects of a product's UI. A guideline for usability test reports is that they highlight positive aspects of the product as well as negative aspects; heuristic evaluation reports can also highlight the major positive aspects of a product. Listing the positive aspects of a product has several advantages:

- Evaluation reports that highlight positive and negative issues are perceived as more balanced by the product team.
- You might reduce the likelihood that something that works well is changed for the worse.
- You may want to propagate some of the positive design features throughout the product.
- Sometimes the positive features being mentioned actually bring focus to some of the very negative features being highlighted.

Individual Reliability and Group Thoroughness

The unreliability of individual problem reports, where different individuals report different problems, is well documented and is the rationale for having multiple inspectors. Hartson, Andre, and Williges (2003) point out that attempts to standardize inspection processes (by including detailed tasks and procedures, for example) might improve the reliability of multiple inspectors but reduce the thoroughness of the group results by "pointing all the inspectors down the same path" (p. 168).

DATA, ANALYSIS, AND REPORTING

The primary data from a heuristic evaluation are a list of problems, each categorized as follows:

- Location in the UI
- A description of the problem

- Which heuristics are associated with the problem
- The number of evaluators who found the problem. The type of evaluator (e.g., usability practitioner versus developer versus domain expert)
- Whether the problem is a global issue (it appears in many places in the product) or a local problem that is confined to a single location (Dumas & Redish, 1999)
- Severity rating from each evaluator to assist in prioritization of problems (rating can be the result of discussion and consensus or an average of the individual ratings).

Given that heuristic evaluations are meant to be efficient, the immediate analysis is generally a list of problems that are prioritized by criteria important to the product team (e.g., severity, cost, difficult to implement). The "keeper" of the data from heuristic evaluations and other sources of usability problem data can track data over time and examine the data for patterns:

- Are particular heuristic being violated often?
- Are severity ratings becoming more consistent over time?
- Who are the best evaluators?
- Do evaluators find different problems as a result of their role or experience?
- Are the particular areas of a product where more problems than expected are being found?
- Do you need to consider additional heuristics?

Yahuda and McGinn (2007) presented the results of a heuristic evaluation of eight websites by defining "usability expectations" for features of interest (e.g., contact information). The intent of this research was to determine which solutions for features across the eight sites were the best based on how well the solutions met usability expectations. These usability expectations were based on a set of heuristics and were focused on the domain of interest. Each usability expectation was assigned a value based on a maximum of 5 points. Evaluators rated a set of designated features by assigning points to the usability expectations. This method can be used for example, to rate a "Directions" feature. The Directions feature might receive 1 point for being usable on a small screen, 1 point for having text that is readable, 1.5 points for clear verbal driving instructions from your location, 1 point for simplicity (not too much detail), and 0.5 points for providing useful landmarks—for a total of 5 points. The sum of the points for each feature in the Yehuda and McGinn study was reported on a five-star rating. Features that met all usability expectations were rated as ★ ★ ★ ★ ★ . Features that met around 60% of the usability expectations received a ★ ★ ★ rating. Features that failed to meet most or all of the expectations got a ★ rating (an "awful") solution. The star ratings as well as the ratings for each usability expectation provided quick assessments of feature usability as well as the details behind the star ratings.

One of the questions that you might want to consider is "How do you measure the success of a heuristic evaluation?" In the usability literature, the focus is generally on how many problems of various severities are found. That is a start, but a more important measure might be how many problems are fixed. Sawyer, Flanders, and Wixon (1996) suggest that the results of heuristic evaluations and other types of inspections look at the impact ratio which is the ratio of the number of problems that the product team commits to fix divided by the total numbers of problems found times 100 (p. 377). While the impact ratio provides a measure of how many problems are fixed, this measure still does not indicate how much more usable the product is as a result of the identified and fixed problems.

CONCLUSIONS

The heuristic evaluation method has received much attention since it first emerged in the early 1990s as a discount usability technique. The technique can be used by an individual or a multidisciplinary team. This chapter highlighted both the strengths and weaknesses of the heuristic evaluation method and also provided numerous tips for improving the quality of heuristic reviews. With appropriate training, examples, and knowledge of users, tasks, and environments, heuristic evaluation will be a useful tool for user experience practitioners.

CHAPTER 2

The Individual Expert Review

Alternative Names: Expert review, UI inspection.

Related Methods: Heuristic evaluation, cognitive walkthrough, perspective-based inspection.

OVERVIEW OF THE INDIVIDUAL EXPERT REVIEW

Research cited in the HCI and UX literature cautions that a single individual who reviews a UI is likely to miss many problems (Hertzum et al., 2002; Nielsen, 1992). However, many practitioners are, nonetheless asked to do an expert evaluation of a product, often on short notice with no budget for testing or heuristic evaluations with multiple inspectors. This chapter provides a general procedure and tips on how a lone employee or consultant can do a credible job finding usability problems when asked to deliver an individual expert usability review.

To optimize an individual expert review, a lone practitioner can examine any existing data about a product or service (e.g., feedback from beta testing, technical support calls, and user forums), use personas to understand the goals and pain points of users, conduct an individual walkthrough, interview a few users of the product or prototype, review the product against common heuristics, principles, and patterns, and examine the product from different perspectives.

When the term "expert" is used in the HCI literature, it can refer to several types of expertise:

- **HCI and usability expertise**. Do you have experience with a variety of HCI methods as well as actual usability evaluation experience?
- **Product genre expertise**. Do you have general experience or specific testing experience with the type of product or service you will be evaluating?
- **Specific product expertise**. Have you worked with a previous or current version of the product or service you are asked to evaluate?
- **Domain expertise**. Do you have knowledge of the concepts, terminology, and work practices that are used in domains such as content management, network performance monitoring, chemical analysis, and architectural design?
- **User and environment expertise**. Do you have experience with users and the range of environments involved? There are many situations where new employees do not have much exposure to users for weeks, months, or even years after they begin working with the product. With mobile hardware and software evolving quickly, you might need to understand what it is like to use an app on busy streets, at a construction site, in a call center, or in the snow.

- **Business expertise**. Do you understand the business goals the product is trying to satisfy? Business goals might include increase customer loyalty, reduce support calls, increase the return on investment (ROI), grow market share, be the innovation leader, persuade people to buy something, and increase the level of positive sentiment toward your product or company in social media. Seek out the business goals for your company, organization, division, and team and make sure that you consider these goals in your exert evaluation. If your company has decided that it needs to upgrade its visual image, then aesthetics might be one focus of your expert review.

As a rough generalization, the more expertise you have in each of these categories, the more problems and issues you will identify in your individual expert review. However, several factors in addition to expertise can affect the results of an individual expert review.

- **Your credibility (especially in a new position)**. For individual expert reviews, it is often necessary to prove that your opinion is "better than anyone else's opinion" before your review carries more weight than other individuals. If you are new in a position (consultants face this often, but a new job or a corporate acquisition can also create the situation), there are several things you can do to improve your credibility. First invest time understanding the product. Take courses, read user forums, use the product yourself as much as possible, keep notes, learn the vocabulary (this author often develops a set of "flash cards" with new terms, concepts, and features). Getting up to speed quickly in a new area is a good way to accelerate your credibility with product team members.
- **Conflicts of interest**. If you are involved in design as well as evaluation and are, in effect, evaluating something that you helped to design, you have a conflict of interest that could blind you to some problems or affect your perception of the seriousness of problems.
- **Social pressure**. While there are ways to soften the results of an expert review (noting good features as well as problems), you have to continue working with the colleagues whose work you are evaluating, and the desire to have a positive relationship can consciously or unconsciously influence your results.

- **Lack of clear limits on what to evaluate**. This author once had 500 screenshots dumped in his office with an order to "make this better" and have the report ready in two weeks. It took much longer than two weeks (more like two years) to really make things better.
- **Corporate taboos**. One of the most difficult circumstances for an HCI practitioner occurs when there is some fundamental flaw with a product that affects the UX (and everyone is aware of this), but discussion of the flaw is considered a taboo topic by management (Schrage, 2000). For example, an ancient database or old (and possibly bad) UI architecture could be at the core of user complaints about a product, but because fixing the legacy code requires tremendous effort and a dry spell for revenues, the root cause of the fundamental problem is off-limits for discussion.

This chapter describes how an HCI or usability practitioner, working alone, can find problems and issues during an individual expert review of a product, website, or service. Although this chapter focuses on how to improve the quality of an individual expert review, practitioners should, when time, budget, and resources are available, employ multiple reviewers and complementary methods, such as heuristic evaluations and user testing, to supplement their individual expert reviews.

STRENGTHS

The individual expert review has the following strengths:

- You don't need a usability lab, recruiter, participants, or extensive funding to do an individual expert review.
- You can devise a custom procedure for evaluation that maps to your experience, the UX goals, and the business goals.
- You can conduct an individual expert review early in development and highlight potential problems. You can begin with an inspection of the functional/UI specifications and continue until the product is ready to ship.

WEAKNESSES

The individual expert review has the following weaknesses:

- Single reviewers may generate false positives (problems that aren't really problems) that can hurt credibility, especially if a team spends time fixing things that weren't really broken. To avoid this, usability practitioners can employ the principle of triangulation (focus on problems that occur across methods, users, and tasks).

- A single reviewer is likely to miss some major and minor problems. A single reviewer is unlikely to uncover even a majority of usability problems in any typical product (Hertzum et al., 2002).
- Lack of domain or HCI expertise can limit the individual evaluator's effectiveness and result in many missed problems. If the reviewer misses a key problem that later requires substantial rework, the reviewer's credibility will suffer.
- Individuals may feel more confidence in their results than is warranted.
- Unless the evaluator has high credibility, the report may be viewed as "one person's opinion" and discounted even when it indicates some serious, real problems. Note that you might be able to counteract this weakness if you know of other sources (surveys and product reviews) that reveal the same problems.
- You could have "blind spots" in your review if you are involved in the development of the product. The longer you have experience with a product, the more difficult it is to understand how new users might interact with it.

WHAT DO YOU NEED TO USE THE INDIVIDUAL EXPERT REVIEW?

This section provides a brief description of the basic resources needed to conduct an individual expert review.

Personnel, Participants, and Training

An individual expert review involves a single practitioner who is asked to provide feedback on the usability of a UI. In this method, there is usually no formal usability testing or extended interaction with users, although informal interviews and testing are recommended to strengthen the results. The expert reviewer should have a strong grasp of usability and design principles as well some domain experience.

Hardware and Software

Beyond access to the particular product or prototype, this method needs no special hardware or software beyond a basic set of tools for creating documents and diagrams.

Documents and Materials

These documents and materials can be used for this method.

A review plan describes the following:

- The product that is to be reviewed
- The business and UX goals
- What you need from the product team (access to prototypes, a technical person for questions, specifications, access to the bug database, etc.)
- The major questions the product team has about the product
- The degree of coverage of the review (how many screens, pages, windows, dialog boxes, sections of documentation)
- Any general heuristics or domain-specific guidelines that will be used
- User profiles or personas that provide descriptions of the major user groups
- Core tasks
- Areas of the product that are new
- The schedule
- The scale that you will use to provide a first estimate of the severity or priority of the problem
- A description of the deliverable from your review with a sample of your final report, along with feedback on the format of the final report to make sure that it fits the needs of the product team.

●●●

Using a Single Table to Sort Problems by Different Criteria

If there is no formal template in your organization for recording usability problems and you are using a document file or spreadsheet (e.g., Microsoft Word, Excel, or Google Documents), one trick to consider is putting all your problems in one giant table. If you do this, you can sort by any column and also add a column if you need to sort on a new variable. For example, you can add a column in which you enter an "L" for local problem and a "G" for global problem after you do your review and then sort so that the "Gs" (global problems that came up across the product) are at the top. You can then re-sort by severity or by location in the product.

PROCEDURES AND PRACTICAL ADVICE ON THE INDIVIDUAL EXPERT REVIEW METHOD

The following procedures are meant for the solo practitioner who is asked to provide a usability review or inspection of a product.

The goal of the procedures and advice is to suggest ways to increase the number and quality of usability problems and issues that you can find when working on your own with limited contact or input from users or other colleagues.

These procedures come both from personal experience and from research that focuses on techniques for finding usability problems. Although the suggestions in this chapter are designed to improve the odds of finding usability problems when working alone, it is important for individual reviewers to understand that they are unlikely to find all the usability problems within a particular UI representation.

If the product you are working on is complex (e.g., controls and displays for nuclear power plants, chemical plants, architectural design software, or medical devices) with significant risks for users and other stakeholders, your review can be a starting point but you need to involve multiple evaluators, supplement your review with other forms of testing and evaluation, and domain experts, and use more rigorous evaluation methods.

Planning and Developing the Individual Expert Review Method
Follow these steps to plan and develop an individual expert review:

1. **When you are asked to review a product under development, do some research to understand your users, tasks, environments, the current product (if there is one), and your major competitors**. If you can't visit some customers, then talk with support teams, read user forums on similar products, and search blogs that might be relevant. Interview colleagues or clients in technical support and quality assurance (QA) about common support calls for the current or related products. Have them perform a walkthrough of the product highlighting key issues (e.g., which aspects of the current interface result in the most support calls). Short interviews with QA, training, tech support, and if available, field representatives, can often significantly enhance your review. If you are new to a domain or product, these interviews are even more critical to accelerate your learning curve and allow you to go beyond surface problems.
2. **Do brief, informal usability interviews with a few users of the current product, similar products, or directly competitive products if possible**. If you can't find actual users, look for surrogate users such as trainers, sales support engineers, and marketing representatives.

This method assumes that you don't have the resources for any formal usability testing.

3. **See if there are any good references that can help you understand the domain better**. For example, if you were asked to review a hotel reservation system from the perspective of the desk clerks, you might want to examine trade publications that discuss the issues faced by desk clerks during the holiday season.

4. **Search for articles on competitive products, and make a list of the issues discussed in those articles**. These articles might be in magazines that focus on particular types of software such as mobile apps, professional journals, or reports from groups, such as Forrester or Gomez. One technique is to find as many reviews as possible about a particular product or class of product (say job sites such as Monster.com, HotJobs, and ComputerJobs.com) and list all the usability-related issues that emerge from the reviews. These issues can be used as prompts or "heuristics" for your individual expert review.

5. **Create a checklist of heuristics, best principles, critical questions, and specific issues based on the research that you have done**. This is a mnemonic aid and not necessarily something that you will check off as you proceed with your review.

6. **Create a set of relevant tasks based on all your research, and determine which UX attributes (e.g., learnability, efficiency, satisfaction, readability) are most important**. See the sidebar on UX attributes.

●●● ───

UX Attributes to Consider During an Individual Expert Review

The attributes that make for a good UX vary by product. For a product that you use once a year for national taxes, you want high *learnability* and solid *error prevention*. For a mobile app used to track construction, you might focus on *usefulness*, *efficiency*, *flexibility*, and *evolvability*. If you were reviewing the design for a web-based watch store, you might want to focus on *learnability* issues because people won't likely be coming back repeatedly. If you were reviewing an integrated development environment for C++, you might want to consider *efficiency* as the more critical attribute given the pressure to produce code. Understanding what attributes are most critical to users is a critical skill for the individual evaluator (Wixon & Wilson, 1997). Here are some common UX attributes:

- First impressions
- Satisfaction or likability
- Usefulness

- Learnability (initial performance)
- Efficiency (long-term performance)
- Error prevention/error protection
- Readability
- Memorability (ease of remembering after a period of disuse)
- Degree of challenge (for games or entertainment)
- Advanced feature usage
- Flexibility (the extent to which the product can be applied to different kinds of tasks)
- Evolvability (how well does the system adapt to changes in user expertise).

Conducting an Individual Expert Review

An individual expert review can combine aspects of heuristic evaluations, perspective-based inspections, cognitive walkthroughs, informal usability testing, and other evaluation methods. This section provides a general approach that you can modify to suit the particular state of your product (current product; specification for new product; low-, medium-, or high-fidelity prototype) within time and resource constraints. The procedures assume that the review time is from two to ten days and the product is of moderate complexity, but can be adapted for other degrees of complexity.

1. **Consider a totally uninformed review of the product before you talk with any stakeholders, read any literature, or apply any tasks specified by the product team (Krug, 2009).** You only have one chance to experience the product as a naïve user untouched by the political or technical concerns of stakeholders. Buley (2013) recommends a technique called the "heuristic markup" where you use a product from start to finish (or you work through the key tasks if it is not a product that you work through sequentially) and annotate screenshots with your thoughts about how the product meets user goals, follows design principles, and provides a smooth flow. She recommends that you consider putting yourself in the shoes of a persona to better empathize with the actual users and also record your emotions (be cautious here about being too extreme since the annotated screenshots might be seen by others who might object to extreme emotional statements).

2. **Conduct brief interviews with the stakeholders.** Try to understand what issues and aspects of the product they consider important.

Good sources are members of the quality engineering team, trainers (although the number of training groups is diminishing as more training moves to video, forums, and social media), and technical communicators (sometimes called learning content experts).

3. **Review the procedures for getting access to the product**. What issues will the user face in logging in, installing, and setting up the product? Is registration required? How much effort must the user expend to get to the real content or primary features?

4. **Note your first impressions of the initial screen, window, page, or form of the product**. If you are evaluating web pages, you might want to look at the type of issues that Nielsen and Tahir (2002) highlight in their book *Homepage Usability*. The book points out subtle issues that might escape even quite experienced reviewers.

5. **Walk through the core tasks of the product from the perspective of your primary user or persona**. On the first pass, you might adopt the perspective that you don't know much about the product and focus on learnability issues because there are always new users or transfer users. On subsequent passes, you might change your perspective one or more times until you have covered all the common user personas (and perhaps an administrator or maintainer!). Following are some general issues to consider during this part of the individual expert review:

   • **Terminology**. Does the interface use any language that would not be understood by a person new to the domain or the product? Don't assume that jargon and acronyms are well understood by the full range of users.

   • **Information scent**. Do web links provide good cues about what the user will find at the other end of the links?

   • **Task flow**. Does the user experience any obstacles as he or she navigates through the product to accomplish a critical goal (buying a book, signing up for a brokerage plan, finding some important information for a research project)? Is it always clear what to do next? Is it possible to back up or cancel or start over easily? Does the task flow take too few or too many steps? Task flow diagrams are a useful tool for any practitioner, bur especially for the lone practitioner working to understand how a product or service works.

●●●

Tools for Diagramming and Annotating Task Flows

A useful tool for individual expert reviews is a simple task flow diagram that shows how you move through an interface to accomplish a goal. You can create diagrams of tasks and then mark up areas where there are flow problems, insufficient cues about what to do next, and poor feedback about progress through the tasks. There are many tools that you can use, including paper, PowerPoint, Visio, OmniGraffle, and Gliffy (www.gliffy.com).

- **Progress indicators and feedback**. Does the system provide clear evidence that you are progressing toward a goal? The design of progress indicators can influence perceived response time. Is there feedback that the action you just took is correct (and if not, what you can do to recover and move forward)?

6. **If there are automated tools that can reveal potential UX problems, consider running those on the product (this assumes that there is a robust, working prototype available)**. The benefits of automated evaluation tools are speed and coverage. The major risk associated with automated tools is a sense of false security. Automated tools have their limitations. For example, automated accessibility checkers will not reveal all the barriers that users with different disabilities may experience with a website.

7. **Consider a "can you break it?" test (Shneiderman & Plaisant, 2010)**. The can-you-break-it test is a staple of quality testing as well as game design (where users of games try to find fatal flaws). If you are testing hardware, there are sometimes official breakage tests (Can this device survive a fall of three feet onto a hard floor?). A can-you-break-it test for software can reveal many issues with error prevention, error recovery, error messages, and general reliability. If you don't have a working prototype, you can pose questions about particular types of input (e.g., what would happen if you typed a phone number as 5555551212 versus 555-555-1212 or used mixed case in a file name or URL?). Things that you can do in a "can-you-break-it" test include the following:

- Enter various symbols into text fields.
- Type in as many characters as possible in text fields and click an action button such as Submit to see how maxing out the character fields affects error messages and reliability (in the author's

experience from a few years ago, in certain applications, this routinely crashed the system).

- Enter international symbols (ĥ, Ü, Æ) into various text fields.
- Put incorrect information in fields (e.g., you might put in four digits of a five-digit US zip code.
- Try making entries of common items, such as phone number, credit card numbers, and dates in different (but common) formats. For example, you might try entering phone numbers as:
  - 2225551212
  - (222) 555-1212
  - 222.555.1212
  - 222-555-1212.
- Examine error messages that appear when you are doing a "can-you-break-it" test to see if they provide specific instructions. For example, if you enter too many characters for the system to handle, see if the message tells you what the actual limit is. Linderman and Fried (2004) provide some good examples of bad feedback where users have to do repeated approximations until they figure out how many characters are actually allowed.
- If one of the "can-you-break-it" scenarios yields an error message, see if you lose only the offending information or all the information that you entered.
- Change the resolution to the extremes that you expect from your users, and use the product at those extremes.
- Turn off the images if you are using a browser, and see if you can still navigate around the site.
- Evaluate search fields by making purposive errors (Linderman & Fried, 2004):
  - Enter common misspellings.
  - Include punctuation and hyphens (W-2 versus W2).
  - Use singular and plural forms
  - Use alternate spellings ("usable" versus "useable").
  - Try using abbreviations and acronyms.
  - Enter synonyms.
  - Use different cases (atm versus ATM).
  - Enter something guaranteed to give null results to see what guidance the system provides to the user about how to get something other than a null set.
8. Examine the product for visual, interaction, and language inconsistencies.

After the Individual Expert Review

After the review, follow these steps:

1. **Compile** the problems and success stories.
2. **Organize the problems in a way that is accepted by the product team**. For example, you can highlight the most serious problems in an executive summary and then organize individual problems by their location in the product.
3. **Consider whether you want to have a group meeting with the developers and designers to prioritize the results** and discuss recommended solutions to the problems.
4. **Enter the problems into your own problem database or the official bug tracking system** so you can track what gets fixed and what doesn't.
5. **Get a commitment from the developers** about which problems they will fix as one metric of effectiveness.
6. **Validate the changes** with user tests or other evaluation methods whenever possible.

VARIATIONS AND EXTENSIONS TO THE INDIVIDUAL EXPERT REVIEW

This section describes variations and extensions of the individual expert review from personal experience and the research and practitioner literature. Also see variations and extensions from the other chapters in this book as they can also be modified for individual expert reviews.

Categorical Inspections

Kurosu, Matsuura, and Sugizaki (1997) proposed a categorical inspection that involves multiple evaluation sessions with each session focusing on only one category of usability. Kurosu and his colleagues used teams of evaluators, but this same approach can be applied to a single evaluator who focuses on one category of usability (say learnability, efficiency, or aesthetics) at a time rather than trying to keep a larger set of heuristics in mind. This method does require a reviewer to have the resolve to focus on only one category at a time and the patience to review the product over and over from the different perspectives.

MAJOR ISSUES IN THE USE OF THE INDIVIDUAL EXPERT REVIEW

The individual expert review is very common for lone practitioners and consultants. Major issues that practitioners will face are described in the section below.

Telling Colleagues That Your Review Is Not Likely to Find All the Serious Problems

The limitations of individual expert reviews should be clearly described to the sponsor of the review and also be included in any informal or formal report. Keep in mind that by using the procedures and tips in this chapter, you might increase the number of problems that you find, but for any but the simplest system, you will still find only a minority of the usability problems.

Triangulation

Although the UCD literature is clear on the inability of a single person or a single usability evaluation to find all the problems in an interface unassisted, often other sources of data (bug reports, customer feedback, and input from QA) can be used to complement the review or testing data. Many of the sources may be available to a lone practitioner who invests the time to seek them out. Using the results from multiple methods to provide converging evidence about usability problems is sometimes referred to as triangulation (Usability First Glossary, n.d.). For example, if a practitioner does field or phone interviews, an expert review, and searches the technical support database, the issues that show up across all three methods would be considered credible problems that need to be considered in any redesign activities. Table 2.1 shows a simple triangulation table of usability methods and problems. A glance at this table shows that Problems 3, 4, 6, and 7 were found across more than three different evaluation methods, making them serious candidates for consideration. Triangulation is an effective method for examining requirements as well as problems. Rather than problems in the columns, you can put requirements and indicate the sources of each requirement.

DATA, ANALYSIS, AND REPORTING

The primary data from an individual expert review are a list of problems that can be categorized by the following:

Table 2.1 Triangulation Table

Method/ Problems	Problem 1	Problem 2	Problem 3	Problem 4	Problem 5	Problem 6	Problem 7
Individual review	X		X			X	
Internal bug database			X	X		X	X
Technical support database			X	X	X		
Interviews with users		X	X	X			
Usability testing							X
Input from QA interviews			X			X	X
Complaints from customer advisory council report			X		X	X	

- Type of problem (navigation, terminology, consistency, standards violation)
- Location in the UI (the URL, page title, window title, error message title)
- Scope of the problem, whether global (it appears in many places in the product) or local (confined to a single location) (Dumas & Redish, 1999)
- Severity rating to assist in prioritization of problems (rating can be the result of discussion and consensus or an average of the individual ratings)
- Estimated effort to fix the problem (this is often done by the product team).

The report from an individual expert review can contain the following sections:

- A brief description of the method with procedures and limitations.
- A description of the positive aspects of the interface.
- An executive summary that describes any general problems that were found across the product (e.g., a general problem might be the

lack of required field indicators or the lack of feedback on fields that require formatting). These are sometimes referred to as global problems (Dumas & Redish, 1999). The executive summary should also describe any serious local problems (problems that are found in a particular place and not throughout the product) that would have a strong impact on the UX. An executive summary normally deals with the top five to ten most serious problems.

- A detailed listing of all the problems found by the expert reviewer. The particular format can vary, but the most basic list describes the problem, indicates where the problem was found (e.g., on a particular page or dialog box), provides an explanation of why it is a problem, indicates the severity of the problem, and optionally provides a brief recommendation on how to solve the problem. A screenshot showing where the problem was found is useful for context; however, long reviews with dozens of screenshots can yield very large and unwieldy files, and might be better provided as an appendix.

CONCLUSIONS

Conducting an individual expert review can be a daunting task especially if you have limited domain or product experience. When you are working as a lone practitioner seek out colleagues and sources of information that can help you accelerate your learning curve. If you can use multiple methods like interviews subject matter experts and first experience testing, you can often deepen and broaden the extent of your review.

CHAPTER *3*

Perspective-Based UI Inspection

Alternative Names: Persona-based inspection.

Related Methods: Cognitive walkthrough, heuristic evaluation, individual expert review, pluralistic walkthrough.

OVERVIEW OF PERSPECTIVE-BASED UI INSPECTIONS

A perspective-based UI inspection requires that one or more individuals evaluate a product's UI from different perspectives (Wilson, 2011). The use of multiple perspectives (similar to role-playing) is meant to broaden the problem-finding ability of evaluators (Virzi, 1997), especially those colleagues with little or no background in usability or UI design.

In perspective-based inspections, the inspectors are generally given descriptions of one or more perspectives to focus on, a list of user tasks, a set of questions related to the perspective, and possibly a set of heuristics related to the perspective (e.g., if one perspective is that of "super-user," you might focus on heuristics related to flexibility, system performance, and efficiency—attributes that a super-user would covet). Inspectors are asked to work through tasks from the assigned perspectives.

Inspectors focus on tasks based on the assigned perspective and list the problems that they found from considering that perspective. For example, if you were looking at something from the perspective of an older or elderly user (Chisnell, Redish, & Lee, 2006), you might highlight issues or problems such as the following:

- Readability of page elements
- Clickable items that are too small or too close together
- Ease of scanning
- Unpredictability of the Back button
- Terminology that may not be easily understood by elderly computer users (what is a URL?)
- Ads that look like parts of the UI and may tell the user that he must "click here to cure viruses" or provide identifying information.

The evaluators are told that they can list any issues or problems they find, but they should conduct their inspection with a strong focus on the particular perspective (or perspectives) they were assigned.

●●●————————————————————————————————

Sidebar: Using Personas to Set Perspective

One way to provide perspective for your inspectors is to provide them with personas along with task and environment information. The personas will each have a different perspective on the product. Chisnell et al. (2006) developed a persona-based technique for evaluating 50 websites. Chisnell and her colleagues developed a set of 20 heuristics that focused on older users and then reviewed the websites using the following procedures:

1. Create expanded personas based on existing personas from the American Association of Retired Persons (AARP).
2. Determine where the personas fall on AARP dimension like Age (50s versus 70s), Ability, Aptitude, and Attitude. The values on these persona dimensions provide evaluators with "user perspectives" as they review their sites.
3. Define high-level tasks based on user research that the personas would perform.
4. Select websites that the personas could use to perform the high-level tasks.
5. Have the evaluators perform the tasks that are appropriate for the websites and record the positive and negative reactions.
6. Rate each observation against the relevant heuristics (for each persona). Chisnell and her colleagues used a 4-point scale for the ratings: 1 = task failure, 2 = serious problem, 3 = minor hindrance, 4 = no problem.

The paper that describes this approach and the heuristics developed for older Web users can be found at: http://www.usabilityworks.net/resources/chisnell_redish_lee_heuristics.pdf.

Desurvire (1994) reported on an evaluation of flowcharts for a voice application where each inspector (from a group of human factors experts, nonexperts, and developers) was asked to review the flowcharts several times, each time taking a different perspective.

The perspectives in Desurvire's study included self (whatever background the reviewer brought), HF expert, cognitive psychologist, behaviorist, sociologist, anthropologist, Freudian psychologist, health advocate, worried mother, and spoiled child. Desurvire found that perspective-based inspections yielded more problems than a heuristic evaluation or cognitive walkthrough, especially for nonexperts. While the results seem promising, this was a preliminary study based on a small sample, and there is no explanation about the choice of perspectives and few details on the procedure.

Zhang, Basili, and Shneiderman (1999) conducted a controlled experiment comparing heuristic evaluation to perspective-based inspections. In their study, participants were asked to review a UI from one of the three perspectives: novice use, expert use, and error handling.

The participants in this experiment were given the following: a description of the web-based application, the user tasks, a description of the perspective, usability questions (some might be called heuristics in question format) related to the perspective (e.g., in the "novice" condition, a usability question was "Are formats for data entries indicated?"), and a usability report form. The investigators found that the perspective-based inspections yielded more usability problems than heuristic inspections and concluded that assigning evaluators specific perspectives leads to improved problem detection, especially for those who are not usability experts.

WHEN SHOULD YOU USE A PERSPECTIVE-BASED INSPECTION?

You can use a perspective-based UI inspection for two specific goals:

- To generate ideas or requirements.
- To find solutions to problems.

The primary goal of a perspective-based UI inspection is to reveal as many usability or design problems as possible at relatively low cost. The secondary goal of the perspective-based UI inspection is to focus attention on a particular area. You can use a perspective-based UI inspection in the following situations:

- You have limited (or no) access to users.
- Your product must appeal to a wide range of users with quite different perspectives.
- You need to produce an extremely fast review and do not have time to recruit participants and set up a full-fledged laboratory study.
- Your evaluators are dispersed around the world.
- You are looking for breadth in your review.

Perspective-based UI inspections can be conducted at any stage of the development cycle (Table 3.1) where there is some representation of the UI (UI or functional specification, detailed storyboards, paper prototypes, or working prototypes). Perspective-based inspections can

Table 3.1 Phases of Development When Perspective-Based Inspections Are Useful				
✓	✓	✓	✓	✓
Problem Definition	Requirements	Conceptual Design	Detailed Design	Implementation

Table 3.2 Relative Effort and Resources Required for Perspective-Based Inspection Development and Use				
Overall Effort Required	Time for Planning and Conducting	Skill and Experience	Supplies and Equipment	Time for Data Analysis
▓▓□□□	▓▓□□□	▓▓□□□	▓□□□□	▓▓□□□

be conducted iteratively (along with other methods) throughout the entire development process to find and filter out usability issues and minimize rework by development.

Table 3.2 illustrates the relative effort required, on an average, to develop and use perspective-based inspections. Many of these require limited resources; however, if your perspective-based inspection is used for high-risk situations, the resources required may increase considerably.

STRENGTHS

The perspective-based inspection has many of the same strengths as the heuristic evaluation (see Chapter 1) and the following additional strengths:

- The use of perspectives in an inspection broadens (at least theoretically) the view of evaluators and allows them to see the interface in different ways that should increase the number of problems they find.
- The perspective-based inspection can be quite fun. This author has found that asking inspectors to take on a new perspective provided both fun and challenge for team members. You can take advantage of your team's expertise, for example, by asking someone with an artistic bent to be the "art critic" and focus on the aesthetics of a product or service.

WEAKNESSES

The perspective-based inspection has many of the same weaknesses of the heuristic evaluation (see Chapter 1) and the following additional weaknesses:

- The research on perspective-based inspections is somewhat limited. There is little guidance on how to choose perspectives or write instructions to ensure that the inspectors actually employ the perspective in their reviews.

• The facilitator has to provide enough background for evaluators to understand and apply a particular perspective. For example, if you ask an evaluator to take the perspective of an eighty-year-old Nobel Prize winner who wants to use the alumni site of an Ivy League university, you might need to point out that a brilliant, elderly genius may still be relatively unsophisticated about, or even dislike, computers.

WHAT DO YOU NEED TO USE THE PERSPECTIVE-BASED INSPECTION?

This section provides a brief description of the basic resources needed to conduct a perspective-based inspection.

Personnel, Participants, and Training

You need a facilitator who coordinates the activities of the evaluation team. The facilitator will prepare the materials, conduct training, arrange for the UI to be available, collect the evaluations, compile and analyze the results, organize a group review if necessary, prepare a report, and develop an inspection infrastructure to track the issues that emerge within and across products.

Facilitators need to be trained in the following:

• How to integrate this method with other usability evaluation methods.
• Who to choose for the evaluation team.
• How to integrate the problems from multiple reviewers.
• How to determine the strengths and weaknesses of the method.
• A method for determining how serious the problems are.

A perspective-based evaluation generally requires a team ranging from two to ten people with a mixture of usability, product, domain, and work experience. Like other types of inspections, the evaluation teams can benefit from some reviewers who are outside the product team to spot problems that might go unnoticed by those who are experienced with the product.

Members of the evaluation team need to be trained in the following:

• How to go about the evaluation (using scenarios, screenshots, etc.).
• Descriptions and explanations of the perspectives used in a particular study.

- Practice looking at the product from a particular perspective.
- How to record problems.
- Hardware or software that will be used.
- Depending on the size of your evaluation team, you may need assistance in compiling and debugging the results (determining if different narrative accounts of the problems are in fact the same problem or different problems). If your perspective-based inspection procedure calls for think-aloud sessions where the inspectors do verbal reviews, you will need notetakers (preferably with some usability and product experience so they provide accurate descriptions of problems).

Hardware and Software

Besides the obvious need to provide the evaluators with the product they are evaluating, you also need to consider the following:

- Online forms for entering problems (word documents, spreadsheets, or forms that put problems directly into a database).
- An audio or video recording if your procedure calls for thinking aloud. This can be optional if your notetaker can keep up with the comments, but at a minimum, consider audiotaping the sessions for those times when you have someone who talks fast and you don't want undue interruptions.
- A database for tracking problems, solutions, fixes, and whether subsequent reviews or testing indicate that the problem is actually fixed. As noted earlier, the number of problems found is a common metric in research, but in the world of the practitioner, the number of problems fixed and subsequent verification that the fix yielded an improvement are the more critical metrics.

Documents and Materials

The following documents and materials are needed for perspective-based inspections:

- A description of the perspectives that the inspectors are to follow.
- Training materials.
- Forms for entering problems (can be online).
- A list of task scenarios that you want reviewers to follow and/or the particular parts of the UI that will be reviewed.
- A catalog of screenshots, wireframes, or the UI/functional specification for the product (if not yet working). Even if you have a

working prototype or product, a catalog of screenshots is a useful way to provide context for the evaluators. It can be quite useful to have a screenshot at the top of a page followed by the problem entry form below.

- Report templates suitable to both executive audiences and to the members of the product team who are responsible for making changes based on the heuristic evaluation.
- A feedback form to find out the inspector's reactions to the perspective-based method.

PROCEDURES AND PRACTICAL ADVICE ON THE PERSPECTIVE-BASED INSPECTION

The next section of this chapter focuses on how to plan and conduct a perspective-based inspection.

Planning and Developing the Perspective-Based Inspection

To plan and develop the inspection, follow these steps:

1. **Choose a team of evaluators**. If the product is complex, and the evaluators do not have much familiarity with the product, consider having a domain specialist work with each evaluator.
2. **Choose a set of perspectives for the inspection team**. The current research does not provide strong guidance on how to choose the perspectives that will yield the largest number of "real" problems. Some factors that you might consider when choosing your perspectives include the following:
   - The frequency of use of the product or service. You might want to consider the perspective of a person who uses your product once a year versus many times a day.
   - The characteristics of your users based on user profiles or personas.
   - Experience levels (novice versus expert user).
   - Specific physical or cognitive limitations.
   - Attitudes toward technology.
   - Usability attributes that are important to the product (error prevention inspector, consistency czar, aesthetic judge, readability assessor).

UX Goals as a Guide to Choosing Perspectives

One approach that has proven useful for this author is to choose perspectives that are related to the UX goals. For example, if you have the goal to provide expert users with an efficient UI, you assign someone the role of efficiency expert and ask that person to consider things such as "too many clicks," "lack of shortcuts," "too much mouse movement," and "whether common tasks can be automated." If learnability is a key goal, you might ask someone to play the "new user" and look for aspects of the UI that either supported or hindered learnability.

3. **For each perspective, define the tasks, the user goals for each task, the important characteristics of the perspective, and a set of questions related to the perspective.** Keep in mind that the level of task detail you provide for the evaluators may affect what problems emerge.
4. **Plan and conduct a short training session (one to two hours) with potential evaluators**. The amount of time will dictate the details of your training, but here is a general set of activities to consider:
   * Provide an overview of the method.
   * Provide a detailed description of the perspectives that you are asking your inspectors to use.

An Example of a Perspective for a Review of an Alumni Website

Here is a perspective that I've used when my team did not have a visual designer.

Visual Design Expert: In the review of the alumni site, our goal is to make it attractive as well as useful. In the review of the prototype site, we would like you to take the perspective of a visual design expert and review the product for aesthetics. We want you to consider visual issues like the layout of controls on the screen, the use of colors, the clarity and professionalism of the icons, the use of grids, and consistency with principles of visual design like symmetry, proximity, grouping, contrast, and visual flow. Note any place in the UI where you see visual inconsistencies. Look for any words in labels that are superfluous. Consider images that fit the philosophy of the new site. You can think of yourself as an art critic and visual designer. Consider whether any visual aspects of the site might impede accessibility for someone with low vision.

- Conduct a practice walkthrough of the recommended procedure. Prepare examples of how you want the problems to be reported.
- Conduct a hands-on exercise where each person uses his or her assigned perspective (or perspectives if you want people to use more than one) to evaluate a portion of a UI. The exercise should use the same representation (e.g., paper sketches) of the UI that will be used in the actual exercise.
- Field any questions that emerge.

Conducting the Perspective-Based Inspection

To conduct the inspection, follow these steps:

1. **Provide the inspection team with the materials required for the evaluation of the particular representation of the UI that is available (a catalog of screenshots, a paper prototype, a set of wireframes with clickable links, a working prototype, or even a competitive product)**.
   - Review the procedures briefly with the entire team if possible and field any questions.
   - Go over the schedule for the inspection and be explicit about when their problem reports are due. Provide any passwords and access information.
   - Ask the evaluators to conduct individual evaluations of the UI without communicating with each other.
2. **Ask your evaluators to list problems separately, even if the same problem recurs in different places in the UI (global problems can be identified during the analysis and reporting phase)**.
3. **Collect the problem reporting forms containing the list of problems found by each evaluator**.

After the Perspective-Based Inspection

After the inspection, follow these steps:

1. **Compile the individual lists of problems into a single list that you can sort easily**. If you asked your evaluators to rate the severity of the problems, average the ratings for the same problem. Or, perhaps an easier route is to ask the evaluation or product team to rate the severity of the problems from the master list (after the redundancies are eliminated).

2. Consider whether you want to have a group meeting of the evaluators, developers, and designers to discuss the results, prioritize the problems, and consider potential solutions to the problems.
3. Enter the problems into your own problem database or the official bug tracking system so you can track what gets fixed and what doesn't.
4. Get a commitment from the developers about which problems they will fix. This is one metric of effectiveness.
5. Validate the changes with user tests or other evaluation methods whenever possible.
6. Get feedback on the method and your report on the inspection results as part of a process-improvement plan.

VARIATIONS AND EXTENSIONS TO THE PERSPECTIVE-BASED INSPECTION METHOD

This section describes variations and extensions of the perspective-based inspection method from the research and practitioner literature.

Persona-Based Inspections

The use of personas is common in the UX field. Personas can be used in inspections and walkthroughs as a guide to how users might interact with a product. Pruitt and Adlin (2005) describe how to use personas in informal reviews. Members of a team ask questions about the interface from the perspective of the persona. Markopoulos, Read, MacFarlane, and Hoysniemi (2008) provide some examples of how personas can be used to review children's products.

The Structured Heuristic Evaluation Method

Kurosu et al., (1997) proposed a variation on the heuristic evaluation called the structured heuristic evaluation method (sHEM) that shares some similarities with a perspective-based UI inspection. The sHEM involves multiple evaluation sessions with each session focusing on one category or attribute of usability and a set of associated heuristics that define each category. The categories of usability in Kurosu's sHEM are listed here:

- Ease of cognition (part 1).
- Ease of operation.
- Ease of cognition (part 2).
- Pleasantness.

- Novice versus expert users.
- Users with special care (this category dealt with very young and elderly users; users who had visual, hearing, or physical disabilities; left-handed users; and color-blind users).

Cognitive efficiency was the rationale for focusing on only one category of usability during a session. Kurosu and his colleagues felt that trying to keep many heuristics in mind while reviewing a product was difficult for evaluators. Subcategories with heuristics under each category provide focus for the evaluation team.

At the end of the thirty-minute inspection, there is a fifteen-minute break, and then the team begins a new thirty-minute review using a new category. This is repeated until the team has gone through all the six usability categories. At the end of the session, there is a group meeting where all the inspectors present their problems and then group them into related topics.

Kantner, Shroyer, and Rosenbaum (2002) used an sHEM to conduct inspections of documentation. Like Kurosu, Kantner and her colleagues had usability categories, evaluation dimensions (subcategories), and heuristics that focused the efforts of evaluators (Table 3.3).

The sHEM process followed by Kantner and her colleagues involved the following steps:

1. Recruit an evaluation team. As in any form of product inspection, you want multiple evaluators.
2. Gather information about users, their jobs, their tasks, product functionality, and concerns of the product team.
3. Identify tasks where users are seeking information. The tasks might involve both hardcopy and online documentation.
4. Develop a list of usability categories, evaluation dimensions, and heuristics like those found in Table 3.3.
5. Decide how many sessions and which categories and dimensions you will cover during each evaluation session.
6. Evaluate key pages of the documentation using the tasks and heuristics. List issues and problems that emerge and rate their severity. Indicate where you found the problem.
7. Discuss the issues with the evaluation team and decide which issues to pursue in this version and which to deal with in the future.

Table 3.3 Example of Inspection Categories from Kantner et al. (2002)				
	Evaluation Dimensions			
Criteria Category	**Structure**	**Presentation**	**Dynamics**	**Content (Not the Focus)**
1. Orientation	The user: • Knows how to get to all the information about a topic. • Knows his/her place within the information structure. • Can determine where a search result is in the document structure.	• Primary-related topics are easy to distinguish from tangential-related topics.	The user: • Can get back to previous location. • Can hold current place while checking other information.	
2. Efficiency	• Frequently sought information is located at high levels of the structure. • Within headings, the most important words come first. • Layered information and branching provide minimalist paths through information.	• Related-information links are positioned where they are most easily noticed.	• The user can navigate quickly to the last item, first item, any items, and selected item. • Commonly performed operations require no more than two clicks. • The user can easily identify how to access online help or the online manual.	
3. Flexibility		• The same information can appear in different views depending on context.	• Several paths are provided to the same information: context sensitivity, index with alternative terms, contents that reflect user's place, related-topics links, and maps. • Simple and advanced searching is available.	

MAJOR ISSUES IN THE USE OF THE PERSPECTIVE-BASED INSPECTIONS METHOD

The perspective-based inspection is a novel approach for many UX practitioners. Some of the major issues that practitioners will face are described in the section below.

What Perspectives Should I Use?

Current literature provides little guidance on this issue. The perspectives can be based on many things, including general usability categories, user attributes, and specific roles. For example, this author facilitated a perspective-based inspection of a university alumni website where evaluators from the university with domain, technical, and usability experience were asked to evaluate the site from multiple perspectives based on user profiles, personas, and important usability attributes such as consistency and accessibility. Here are the perspectives used by this author:

- **Consistency enforcer**. Consistency was viewed as a critical attribute for the product so one person was focused on any type of visual or interaction consistency.
- **Visually disabled individual**. The site needed to be accessible by students who were blind or had limited vision.
- **Bad typist**. The site had many forms for registering for events and some alumni who were one-finger typists.
- **QA engineer**. This perspective focused on quality issues such as performance, error messages, and typos.
- **Novice to the web**. In this study, we assumed that some of the older users would not be web savvy so one person was asked to imagine that she had never used the web before.
- **Expert user**. This perspective reflects those who disliked waiting or encountering obstacles in the site that slowed them down.
- **Aesthetics monitor**. This perspective looked for clutter, bad graphics, and poor visual design.

The perspectives were chosen to cover a range of usability attributes, including accessibility, novice use, expert use, consistency, aesthetics, branding, use of graphics, and error handling and prevention. The inspectors were asked to work through a set of tasks and then explore the product with a focus on the assigned perspective, although they could report on any issue, not just the ones associated with the perspective. Issues and questions to consider were discussed for each perspective. The "bad typist" was chosen to see what it would be like for a poor typist to fill in a number of forms. The QA engineer, for example, focused on actions that might result in errors (typing in odd characters, using a hyphenated name in a form, places where the system did not describes how to enter phone or credit card data, and what happened when errors were made). A side effect of this perspective, in addition to some useful usability conclusions, was the discovery of some buggy fields that caused the system to crash when too many characters were entered.

DATA, ANALYSIS, AND REPORTING

The data and results from a perspective-based UI inspection are a list of problems very much like those of heuristic evaluations. The one difference would be that you have the perspectives as a factor in the evaluation. You could indicate which problems are found by which perspectives. For more details on data, analysis, and reporting, see the last section of Chapter 1 on heuristic evaluation.

CONCLUSIONS

The perspective-based inspection is a method for an individual practitioner or a product team that can expand problem-finding capabilities by using perspectives as usability enhancers. If you take the perspective of an elderly novice user, you may be more likely to consider small text, low contrast, poor accessibility for disabilities, and jargon as poor usability. This method can be fun, cost-effective, and a way to expand the meaning of usability for your colleagues.

BIBLIOGRAPHY

Kantner, L., Shroyer, R., and Rosenbaum, S. (2002). Structured heuristic evaluation of online documentation. *Proceedings of IEEE international professional communication conference (IPCC 2002)* (Portland, OR, USA, September 17–20, 2002).

Cognitive Walkthrough

Alternate Names: Simplified cognitive walkthrough, informal cognitive walkthrough.

Related Methods: Heuristic evaluation, perspective-based inspection, pluralistic walkthrough.

OVERVIEW OF THE COGNITIVE WALKTHROUGH

The cognitive walkthrough is a usability walkthrough technique that focuses primarily on the ease of learning of a product. A cognitive walkthrough can involve a single evaluator or a group of evaluators. In this author's experience, most cognitive walkthroughs involve a small group of usability experts and a few additional members from the product team.

The cognitive walkthrough is based on a theory that users often learn how to use a product through a process of exploration, not through formal training courses (Polson & Lewis, 1990). The cognitive walkthrough was originally designed to evaluate "walk-up-and-use" interfaces (e.g., museum kiosks, postage machines in public places, and ATM machines) but has been applied to more complex products (CAD systems, operating procedures, software development tools) that support new and infrequent users (Novick, 1999; Wharton, Bradford, Jeffries, & Franzke, 1992). The cognitive walkthrough is based on the concept of a hypothetical user and does not require any actual users, in contrast to the pluralistic walkthrough and think-aloud usability testing methods.

The cognitive walkthrough has gone through several versions and many extensions (Mahatody, Sagar, & Kolski, 2010). The original version, referred to here as CW Version 1 (Lewis, Polson, Wharton, & Riemen, 1990), was viewed as requiring substantial background in cognitive psychology (Wharton, Rieman, Lewis, & Polson, 1994) and cumbersome to apply in real-world environments. A second version, CW Version 2, tried to simplify the cognitive walkthrough method for practitioners who were not cognitive psychologists by using more detailed forms and instructions. However, these changes made the cognitive walkthrough procedure too laborious (and nearly as complex as Version 1) for most practitioners. The 1994 version (Wharton et al., 1994), CW Version 3, was written as "a practitioner's guide" and considered the primary reference for those who wanted to learn and conduct cognitive walkthroughs. However, even the practitioner's guide was sometimes viewed as too laborious for fast-paced commercial environments. Spencer (2000) proposed an even more simplified version, SCW, the "streamlined cognitive walkthrough" for fast-paced development. This chapter focuses primarily on Versions CW3 and SCW of the cognitive walkthrough. Later in this chapter, a variation on this method called the "informal cognitive walkthrough" (ICW) is described, which is adapted to agile development environments.

WHEN SHOULD YOU USE THE COGNITIVE WALKTHROUGH?

The cognitive walkthrough can be used during any phase of the development process but is most suited to the design stage where a functional specification and other design documents that provide enough information for the creation of action sequences (user inputs and system responses) for a set of tasks (Table 4.1). Cognitive walkthroughs can be conducted using textual descriptions of action sequences, sketches, paper prototypes, high-fidelity prototypes, and working products.

Table 4.2 illustrates the relative effort required, on average, to develop and use the cognitive walkthrough.

Table 4.1 Phases of Development When Cognitive Walkthroughs Are Useful				
	✓	✓	✓	✓
Problem Definition	Requirements	Conceptual Design	Detailed Design	Implementation

Table 4.2 Relative Effort and Resources Required for Cognitive Walkthrough Development and Use				
Overall Effort Required	Time for Planning and Conducting	Skill and Experience	Supplies and Equipment	Time for Data Analysis
▪▪▪▫▫	▪▪▪▫▫	▪▪▪▫▫	▪▫▫▫▫	▪▪▪▫▫

STRENGTHS

The cognitive walkthrough has the following strengths:

- The cognitive walkthrough does not require a working product or even users.
- The cognitive walkthrough can be applied during any phase of development in which there is sufficient information to describe what users do and what the system does.
- The cognitive walkthrough provides detailed information based on cognitive theory that can be used to formulate specific solutions to problems.
- The cognitive walkthrough has well-defined procedures, is task-based, and focuses on one particular usability attribute, learnability.

●●●
_____

Learnability Comes in Different Varieties

The cognitive walkthrough has a focus on initial usability—walk-up-and-use learning. Initial learning is one type of learnability (Grossman, Fitzmaurice, & Attar, 2009), but there are other types of learnability as well:

- **Learnability over time**. This deals with the impact of practice on errors and task performance.
- **First-time performance with instructions**. This type of learning is what people encounter with yearly national tax software programs or a voice-operated prescription refill service, which provides substantial embedded coaching to its users.
- **Expert learning**. How do experts in a domain learn new tools? How do experts on a tool learn how to use a new tool in the same domain? Many complex systems are not the ones that you can walk up and explore. Some systems (e.g., enterprise resource planning (ERP) and customer relationship management (CRM)) require days of training before anyone is allowed to touch a system.
- **Memorability**. How do users remember skills and knowledge over time?
- **Team learning**. With the future of computing quickly moving toward global collaboration, understanding how people learn to work in teams is becoming a critical issue in UX.

So, if you are asked to improve the learnability of a product, probe deeper with your team, client, or sponsor about just what kind or kinds of learning you need to consider.

_____

WEAKNESSES

The cognitive walkthrough has the following weaknesses:

- The cognitive walkthrough has a narrower focus than other inspection methods such as heuristic evaluation. The focus is on learning and not efficiency or other usability attributes (although in practice, issues other than learnability are often captured).
- The method is laborious and slow, and coverage is often limited to a relatively small number of tasks. Rowley and Rhoades (1992) developed a method called the "cognitive jogthrough" in response to complaints from a development team that the cognitive walkthrough approach did not cover enough tasks to be cost-effective.
- Some complex products, such as the popular design tool, Photoshop™, or other content creation tools such as AutoCAD™,

allow many paths to the same goal. In the cognitive walkthrough, the walkthrough leader must choose the "appropriate" paths to achieve particular goals. Given the sheer number of tools and alternative ways to do things, there could be dozens of paths to accomplish the same goal in a complex product. Take the simple example of bolding text in Microsoft™ Word. You can bold with the keyboard, dialog box, styles, pop-up menus, find and replace, and icons in the ribbon. If your goal was to change all bold text to italics, your path to completing that goal could use any of these methods, although find and replace might be the best one to choose for making changes quickly.

WHAT DO YOU NEED TO USE THE COGNITIVE WALKTHROUGH METHOD?

This section provides a brief description of the basic resources needed to conduct a cognitive walkthrough.

Personnel

The cognitive walkthrough can be conducted by an individual or group. In a group evaluation, these are the important roles:

- **Facilitator**. The facilitator is generally the organizer and maestro of the walkthrough process. The facilitator is responsible for making sure that the walkthrough team is prepared for the session and follows the rules of good meeting management. Wharton et al. (1992) stress that the facilitator must decide when conversations can go beyond the narrow focus of the walkthrough and when those conversations must be reined in.
- **Notetaker**. The notetaker records the output of the cognitive walkthrough.
- **Product expert**. Because the cognitive walkthrough can be conducted early in the design stage (e.g., after requirements and a functional specification), a product expert is desired to answer questions that members of the walkthrough team may have about the system's features or feedback.
- **Evaluators**. Evaluators are representatives from the product team. These representatives can be usability practitioners, requirements engineers, business analysts, developers, writers, and trainers.

Table 4.3 Documents and Material Required for the Cognitive Walkthrough		
Document or Item Name	**Description**	**Required or Optional**
User profile	Description of the primary users who perform the tasks that will be evaluated in a cognitive walkthrough.	Required
Task list	The task list should describe the task in a realistic and concrete manner.	Required
Action sequence for each task in the task list	Novick (1999) provides a good example. He includes the following information: • Date • Analysts • Users • Interface • Task • Action sequence • Comments.	Required
Problem reporting form	This is the form for recording the problems that emerge from the walkthrough.	Required
Representation of the UI	Flip charts, electronic display of outputs from cognitive walkthrough, prototypes, or working features.	Required

Documents and Materials

Table 4.3 lists the required and optional materials for the cognitive walkthrough.

PROCEDURES AND PRACTICAL ADVICE ON THE COGNITIVE WALKTHROUGH METHOD

The next section describes the basic procedures for the cognitive walkthrough method as well as practical tips for practitioners.

Planning a Cognitive Walkthrough

The basic steps in planning a cognitive walkthrough are listed here:

1. **Define the users of the product**. The 1994 practitioner's guide (Wharton et al.) and other articles provide little guidance on just how much you need to know about users before starting a cognitive walkthrough. Wharton et al. (1994, p. 109) use the example "Macintosh users who have worked with MacPaint," but you may want to consider a more robust description of the user. There is quite a difference between someone who has years of experience with various draw/paint tools and the eighty-five-year-old father

who was given a Mac and wants to sketch out the arrangement of flowers in his garden. You could use detailed user profiles or personas to provide a description of the primary users (Adlin & Pruitt, 2010). Different personas might take different paths through a system. If you have multiple personas, you can walk through the system with a focus on the attributes of each persona that could have an impact on how easily they can learn how to perform tasks with the target system.

2. **Determine what tasks and task variants (different ways to do the same task) are most appropriate for the walkthrough.** The theory behind the cognitive walkthrough does not address task selection, and the 1994 practitioner's guide provides little help on selecting the tasks that are most critical to users. The choice of tasks must balance complexity, realism, and the time allocated to the walkthrough. One strong recommendation is that the first task in the walkthrough be relatively simple so the team can learn the method before moving on to longer and more complex tasks. Wharton et al. (1992, pp. 383–384) suggest using realistic tasks that involve the use of several core features of the product. If there are multiple ways to do the same task, consider choosing the task variant that novices are most likely to encounter because the focus of this method is on initial learnability. Since much development is focused on new features, your tasks might be ones that take advantage of the new features in a product.

3. **Develop the ground rules for the walkthrough.** For example, your ground rules for conducting the cognitive walkthrough in a group might include:

- Cell phones should be placed in silent mode.
- No computers, smartphones, or tablets for the walkthrough participants. Only the notetaker and presenter will have a computer.
- There will be no design discussions during the walkthrough. The purpose of the walkthrough is to elicit potential learning problems—redesign will generally take place at subsequent sessions. This can be a difficult rule, so you might provide cards where participants can jot down ideas for design solutions and collect those for later design activities.
- Designers will not defend their designs during the walkthrough.
- Participants will be professional and not use derogatory language (e.g., "this is a stupid design for a mobile system that is supposed to be learned in a few moments").

- The facilitator is in charge and will explicitly remind people of the ground rules if a violation occurs.
4. **Generate the action sequences for each task**. An action sequence is a detailed description of the actions the target users must take to complete a task and the associated system responses at each step.

   Here is a simple example of an action sequence that could be reviewed using a target user who is an elderly user with limited computer or web experience. Chrome was installed with the computer.

●●●──

Task: Change the search engine to Bing from Google in the Google Chrome browser using the mouse.
Action Sequence:
1. Click on Chrome icon.
2. The browser appears.
3. Move the mouse pointer to the menu icon in the upper right of the browser.
4. A tooltip appears.
5. Click on the menu icon.
6. The Customize and Control Menu appears.
7. Move mouse pointer to Settings.
8. Click on Settings menu item.
9. Various controls appear in the browser area.
10. Move mouse to the Search drop-down.
11. Click on the drop-down.
12. Three menu items are shown: Google, Yahoo, and Bing.
13. Drag mouse to Bing.
14. Menu item highlights.
15. Click on highlighted Bing menu item.
16. Bing shows up in the drop-down menu field.

──

The granularity of the action sequence is an important consideration (Sears & Hess, 1998). For example, if the user must type some information in a text field, do you count each character as an action or the entire name as an action? The entire name might be considered as a single action on a desktop machine, but perhaps on a mobile device, each character might be considered an action. Another example dealing with task granularity is menu selection. Do you count the selection of a menu item from a pull-down menu as one action (1. Choose Print from the File menu.), two actions (1. Click on File. 2. Click on Print.), or three actions (1. Move pointer to the File menu. 2. Click the File menu name. 3. Click the Print menu item.)? The granularity of actions can differ depending on the likelihood that the users will see an action as an aggregate or a set of subtasks.

5. **Provide a representation of the interface**. This representation can be a detailed text scenario, an operating procedure (Novick, 1999), a set of sketches, a storyboard, a paper prototype, a partially working prototype, or a fully working product.

6. **Assemble a group of evaluators for the cognitive walkthrough**. Candidates include usability practitioners, writers, trainers, product managers, quality engineers, and developers. This author has run cognitive walkthroughs with three to eight team members.

Conducting a Cognitive Walkthrough
To conduct the walkthrough, follow these steps:

1. **Walk through the action sequences for each task from the perspective of the "typical" users of the product**. For each step in the sequence, see if you can tell a credible story using one of three approaches:
   - The four-question approach of Wharton et al. (1994, p. 106):
     - Will the user try to achieve the right action?
     - Will the user notice that the correct action is available?
     - Will the user associate the correct action with the effect that the user is trying to achieve?
     - If the correct action is performed, will the user see that progress is being made toward solution of the task?
   - The ICW of Grigoreanu and Mohanna (2013) where user researchers played the role of users and asked themselves the questions:
     - As the user, would I know what to do at this step?
     - If I do the right thing, as the user, do I know that I have made progress toward this goal?

     After the user researcher walks through the tasks asking one of these sets of questions, other team members join in to provide their comments.

     The second part of the ICW process was a series of pluralistic walkthrough sessions (Chapter 5) where actual users commented on product task flows. So, the ICW is a hybrid method combining the cognitive walkthrough approach with the pluralistic walkthrough.

- The two-question streamlined approach of Spencer (2000):
  - Will the user know what to do at this step?
  - If the user does the right thing, will the user know that he or she did the right thing and is making progress toward the goal?

For each action sequence in a task using the Spencer approach, the moderator (often the designer or usability practitioner) describes the action sequence and the state of the system after the user performs a correct action. Then, the evaluation team attempts to answer the two questions with plausible success or failure stories. If the team can come up with a plausible story for an action sequence, then nothing is recorded. However, if the team can't come up with a plausible success story, then the failure is recorded along with the knowledge that the user must know to progress. If you take the earlier example of an action sequence that required an elderly user to change a search setting, you might consider that there is no plausible success story for the action sequence "move the mouse pointer to the menu icon in the upper right of the browser" because an elderly user using the browser for the first time is not likely to know that the needed menu is represented by three horizontal bars in the upper right of the browser window. The elderly user might look for menus in the more traditional area under the title bar.

A "no" to any of the questions in the three approaches suggests a usability problem.

2. **Record success stories, failure stories, design suggestions, problems that were not the direct output of the walkthrough, assumptions about users, comments about the tasks, and other information that may be useful in design**. Use a standard form for this process so you can easily record and track the information.

After the Cognitive Walkthrough
After the walkthrough, follow these steps:

1. Bring the appropriate stakeholders together to review the results of the cognitive walkthrough.
2. Discuss potential solutions to the UI problems that were found in the walkthrough.
3. Determine which solutions you will apply to the product.
4. Evaluate the cognitive walkthrough process, and determine if there are improvements you could make for subsequent walkthroughs.

VARIATIONS AND EXTENSIONS TO THE COGNITIVE WALKTHROUGH

There are many variations and extensions to the cognitive walkthrough method in the literature. Some of these variations include:

- Heuristic walkthrough. See Chapter 1 for details on this method which is a cross between a heuristic evaluation and a cognitive walkthrough.
- Cognitive walkthrough for the web.
- Groupware walkthrough for highly collaborative systems.
- Cognitive walkthrough with users.
- Distributed cognitive walkthrough.

For a detailed review of eleven variations on the cognitive walkthrough, see the article "State of the Art on the Cognitive Walkthrough Method, Its Variants and Evolutions" by Mahatody et al. (2010). The article provides a description of each type of cognitive walkthrough and also discusses how well the methods support the finding of usability problems.

MAJOR ISSUES IN THE USE OF THE COGNITIVE WALKTHROUGH

Major issues that will face practitioners using the cognitive walkthrough are described in the section below.

How Do Evaluators and Teams Learn to Use the Cognitive Walkthrough Method?

The 1994 practitioner's guide recommends (p. 136) that one person on a walkthrough team has "some basic understanding of cognitive science," but it fails to define just what a "basic understanding" is. Wharton et al. (1994) state that the target audience for their practitioner's guide is "practicing software developers." Few practicing software developers have background in cognitive science so that would be a tough requirement. John and Packer (1995) present a case study of a single computer designer with little training in UX or cognitive science, learning and using the cognitive walkthrough method. They made the following conclusions from this detailed case study:

- The cognitive walkthrough method does not require deep experience with UCD or cognitive science.

- The practitioner's guide should be the primary reference for practitioners. The earlier papers may be too theoretical for the target audience of practicing software developers.

As a UX practitioner, follow this recommended training plan to learn the cognitive walkthrough method:

1. Read this chapter to get an overview.
2. Read the 1994 article and the streamlined method article by Spencer (2000) carefully with emphasis on the examples.
3. If possible, find a mentor who has conducted cognitive walkthroughs or a hands-on seminar or workshop.
4. Conduct several individual cognitive walkthroughs for practice using some simple tasks on a product you are familiar with, and make notes about points in the process where you had problems. Keep a diary and make notes about the process and questions that emerge during your first and subsequent experiences with the cognitive walkthrough (see John & Packer, 1995, for an example of what a diary might contain).

Task Definitions

The cognitive walkthrough does not provide much guidance about choosing tasks (Jeffries, Miller, Wharton, & Uyeda, 1991). The practitioner guide suggests that tasks be chosen on the basis of market studies, needs analysis, and requirements, which is not very helpful, especially at the design stage when there may be many such tasks to choose from. Wharton et al. (1992, p. 387) made some specific recommendations regarding tasks:

- Start with a simple task and move to more complex tasks.
- Consider how many tasks you can complete in a single walkthrough session. A common theme in the research and case study literature is that only a few tasks can be examined in any cognitive walkthrough session. A recommendation is to consider evaluating one to four tasks in any given session depending on task complexity.
- Choose realistic tasks that include core features of the product. Core features are those that form the underpinning of a product. For example, core features in Amazon.com are "search" and "shopping cart."
- Consider tasks that involve multiple core features so you can get input on transitions among the core features.

Other rationales for choosing tasks include the following:

- Whether the task uses new features that are considered high priority by the marketing and product development teams
- How important the task is to a user's first impressions of a product.

There are other factors to consider when choosing tasks for cognitive walkthroughs and other UX methods as listed in Table 4.4.

Table 4.4 Factors to Consider When Choosing Tasks for the Cognitive Walkthrough	
Choose Tasks Based on	**Description**
Requests from your client	Although some clients will hand you a set of tasks to test, be wary because these tasks may only show the product in a good light without revealing core usability problems.
The constraints on your product	The state of the product will dictate possible tasks. Some tasks may not, for example, be possible with a paper prototype or medium-fidelity prototype.
Design team uncertainty	Are there parts of the product about which the design team has reservations or concerns (Wixon & Wilson, 1998)?
Verification of reputed problems	If you have feedback from technical support, articles about your product, or feedback from other sources about a problem, you may want to confirm and explore the problem in more depth in a think-aloud usability test.
Frequency	Tasks that people perform often are good candidates for think-aloud tasks. On the other hand, rare tasks that involve serious consequences also need to be considered.
Criticality	Infrequent tasks that can cause severe problems (lost revenues, catastrophic failure, and physical harm) are candidates for testing.
Important use cases	You can base your tasks on important use cases defined by the product team.
New features	Most product announcements tout new features that make products more "user friendly." Consider testing new features that are likely to have an impact on users or key features that are heavily promoted in the marketing and sales literature.
Avoidance of the confirmatory bias (Stacy & MacMillian, 1995)	The confirmatory bias is a tendency of those who create test cases for products to choose cases that are likely to show that a product works rather than fails. While the research has focused on software development, the same could hold true for usability personnel and is something to keep in mind. Usability personnel may be under subtle pressure to have results that are not too damning to the product.
Edge cases	Consider tasks that involve troubleshooting, error conditions, large databases, slow performance, and other edge cases. Edge cases can reveal problems that may not be evident under

(Continued)

Table 4.4 (Continued)	
Choose Tasks Based on	Description
	"normal" conditions and be quite useful for finding problems that will tax your technical support lines.
Safety or liability concerns	There are examples in the human factors and engineering literature of safety-critical systems such as medical devices, backup software, military systems, and process control systems where a usability team should focus on tasks that are potentially injurious.
Accessibility	Does your system have to support users with various disabilities?

Tedious and Repetitive

A common complaint about the cognitive walkthrough is that the data collection requirements can be repetitive and tedious because you need to answer the same questions for each step in an action sequence. If your action sequence for a single task has twenty-five steps in the action sequence, you will need twenty-five pages to record your data collection. If you also collect design suggestions, assumptions about users, and other "side issues," you can accumulate a considerable quantity of online or paper forms. Here are recommendations for reducing the tediousness of the data collection:

- Record only those actions where there is a problem (a failure) (Wharton et al., 1992).
- Consider automating the data collection using a database with a simple form for input.
- Make any assumptions about the users publicly available during the walkthrough (e.g., record on a flip chart) so you don't have to continually refresh the memory of the evaluation team.
- Avoid "all-day" walkthroughs. Overly long walkthroughs are tiring and sometimes become an obstacle to the development process. Consider short sessions spread over several days.
- The facilitator of the walkthrough must balance the goals of the walkthrough with the goals of the product team. For example, cognitive walkthroughs are generally focused on evaluating the ease of learning of the product and not on solutions to design problems. However, if the discussion seems to be yielding a design solution to a problem that has been holding up the schedule, the facilitator might allow a long enough digression to capture the idea and then move on. And such a discussion might energize the team.

Suboptimal Solutions

The cognitive walkthrough method asks inspectors to record information on user assumptions and knowledge requirements but does not recommend how to use these records (Cockton et al., 2012).

The cognitive walkthrough emphasizes solutions for specific problems encountered in the action sequence of a task but does not deal with more general or higher level solutions that might be applicable across a number of tasks.

DATA, ANALYSIS, AND REPORTING

The primary data from a cognitive walkthrough are learnability problems based on knowledge or skill gaps that would prevent users from completing tasks successfully. Secondary data might include design flaws, or potential solutions (note that the goal is not to have a design session during the walkthrough, but good solutions should be captured). The problem data should be categorized by where in the action sequence it occurred, what user groups were considered, how severe the problem is, the expected frequency of the problem, and whether the problem is local (found in one place) or global (found in multiple places).

CONCLUSIONS

The cognitive walkthrough was designed to focus on exploratory learning and been the object of much research. A number of varieties of the cognitive walkthrough have been proposed to make the process more efficient, with recent "streamlined" and "informal" versions. The cognitive walkthrough is a technique for exposing assumptions about users and learning that can help designers create better first experiences.

CHAPTER *5*

Pluralistic Usability Walkthrough

Alternate Names: Group usability walkthrough.

Related Methods: Cognitive walkthrough, heuristic evaluation, perspective-based inspection.

OVERVIEW OF THE PLURALISTIC USABILITY WALKTHROUGH

The pluralistic usability walkthrough is a group usability evaluation that follows a predefined set of task scenarios. A facilitator presents the participants with an image of the interface for each step in a task. Participants (four to ten representative users) are asked to decide what actions they would take for each step to get to the next step in the task (independently without discussion) and to write those actions down on walkthrough forms containing the screenshots of the UI.

When everyone has written down their actions for a specific step in a task, the facilitator reveals the "correct answer" and invites the group to discuss their answers. The actual users of the product (or the participants who are the closest "surrogate users") speak first and describe their actions for the step, followed by the rest of the walk-through team.

The walkthrough team involves actual users plus some combination of usability practitioners, developers, and other members of a product team. All the participants in the walkthrough are expected to put themselves in the shoes of the user.

WHEN SHOULD YOU USE THE PLURALISTIC USABILITY WALKTHROUGH?

Pluralistic usability walkthrough can be conducted at any stage of the development cycle in which there is some representation of the UI (Table 5.1). The pluralistic usability walkthrough requires, at a mini-mum, a set of sketches or paper prototype showing the "most desir-able" path that a user would follow for each task. The most appropriate time for employing this method is generally during early design (Bias, 1991).

Table 5.2 illustrates the relative effort required, on an average, to develop and use pluralistic usability walkthrough.

Table 5.1 Phases of Development When Pluralistic Usability Walkthrough Are Useful				
		✓	✓	✓
Problem Definition	Requirements	Conceptual Design	Detailed Design	Implementation

Table 5.2 Relative Effort and Resources Required for Pluralistic Usability Walkthrough Development and Use				
Overall Effort Required	Time for Planning and Conducting	Skill and Experience	Supplies and Equipment	Time for Data Analysis
▣▣▢▢▢	▣▣▣▢▢	▣▣▢▢▢	▣▣▢▢▢	▣▣▢▢▢

STRENGTHS

The pluralistic usability walkthrough has the following strengths:

- The method involves actual (or potential) users of the system.
- The method is generally easy to explain to potential participants.
- Participants who have different perspectives that can add to the value of the method.
- Members of the product team get to see the initial impressions of actual users as they walk through key tasks.
- The method is participatory and brings together a product team to hear users and "walk in the shoes of the user." This contrasts with other walkthrough methods (see Chapters 1–3) where users are generally not involved.
- Members of the walkthrough all get to voice their opinions (although the actual users of the product get priority).
- The method addresses both usability problems and possible design solutions.
- The pluralistic usability walkthrough is probably more appropriate for linear tasks where there is a high likelihood of a user following a particular sequence. Tasks where there are many equally likely paths for achieving a goal may not be the best candidates for this method.

WEAKNESSES

The pluralistic usability walkthrough has the following weaknesses:

- A strong facilitator is needed to keep the session on track so discussions don't get bogged down with details, war stories, or lengthy discussions of potential solutions.

- The pluralistic usability walkthrough is not based on any particular cognitive theory.
- Scheduling a diverse group of stakeholders, including actual users, can be difficult.
- The method is relatively slow so the particular tasks chosen must be of high value.
- The thread of tasks must be worked out in advance (Constantine, 1994, p. 400).
- The method focuses more on learning issues than efficiency.
- Preparing the sequence of screenshots for a complex interface and several scenarios can be time-consuming.
- May not be suitable for big picture issues involving multiple tasks and multiple users.

WHAT DO YOU NEED TO USE THIS METHOD?

This section provides a brief description of the basic resources needed to conduct a pluralistic usability walkthrough.

Personnel, Participants, and Training

In a pluralistic usability walkthrough, these are the important roles:

- **Facilitator**. The facilitator is generally the organizer and maestro of the walkthrough process. The facilitator is responsible for making sure that the walkthrough team is prepared for the session and follows the rules of good meeting management. Wharton and her colleagues (1992) stress that the facilitator must decide when conversations can go beyond the narrow focus of the walkthrough and when those conversations must be reined in.
- **Notetaker**. The notetaker records the output of the discussions that emerges during the pluralistic usability walkthrough.
- **Users**. These are actual (or potential) users of the product. Sessions generally involve a single user.
- **Product expert**. Because the pluralistic usability walkthrough can be conducted early in the design stage (e.g., after requirements and a functional specification), a product expert is desired to answer questions that members of the walkthrough team may have about the systems features or feedback. Bias (1994) notes that this person can

serve as "living documentation" because there is often no paper or online documentation available.

- **Internal evaluators**. Three to six representatives from the product team can be usability practitioners, product/project managers, QA engineers, requirements engineers, business analysts, developers, writers, and trainers.

The primary training for a pluralistic usability walkthrough focuses on facilitation skills for the person leading up the walkthrough. Important facilitation skills include the following:

- **Time management**. Pluralistic usability walkthrough generally focus on a limited number of tasks, so it is important to keep the sessions moving while not making the team feel rushed. The speed of the pluralistic usability walkthrough also depends on the pace of the slowest reviewer, so time management is important for the success of the method.
- **Focusing on letting users speak first as the team walks through the steps in a task**. Because the users are generally in the minority and often on the product team's turf, it is important for the facilitators to adhere to the pluralistic usability walkthrough principle of "users first."
- **Keeping the meeting on track and eliminating personal criticism**. The facilitator of a walkthrough must keep side conversations, personal attacks, and personal agendas from occurring in an atmosphere potentially rife with both protectiveness of and frustration with the product.

Documents and Materials

Table 5.3 lists the required and optional materials for the pluralistic usability walkthrough.

Hardware and Software

A computer and projection system can be used to view UI designs in addition to the catalog of screenshots that participants use to mark their comments during the walkthrough.

PROCEDURES AND PRACTICAL ADVICE ON THE PLURALISTIC USABILITY WALKTHROUGH METHOD

The following procedures describe how to plan and conduct a pluralistic usability walkthrough.

Table 5.3 Documents and Forms Required for the Pluralistic Usability Walkthrough		
Document or Item Name	**Description**	**Required or Optional**
A pluralistic usability walkthrough proposal/plan	This is similar to a usability test plan and generally has the following sections: • Purpose and goals • Participants • User tasks • Pretest forms (consent, demographic/background survey) • Walkthrough procedures • Guidelines for observers and participants • Posttest forms or procedures • Limitations of the study • Data analysis and presentation plan • A schedule with a list of deliverables (recruiting plan, test plan, tasks, final report) • Appendices with all forms and walkthrough materials.	A detailed plan is required for the practitioner's first pluralistic usability walkthrough; after that, the plan can be abbreviated.
Consent and nondisclosure documents	The consent form must spell out the participant's rights and describes how the data will be used. A nondisclosure statement can be part of the consent form or a separate document.	Required
Task list with correct actions	The task list should describe the "correct actions" required to complete each task in the pluralistic usability walkthrough. This is used by the facilitator to provide the correct answer at each step.	Required
Reporting form (paper)	The reporting form consists of an image of the UI for a particular step in a task and room to write down what the user would do at this step plus any general comments the user has about the UI. There is a form for each step (change in the UI) in a task. The participants need one set of problem forms for each task in the walkthrough. A session requires one set of forms for each task.	Required
Post-walkthrough questionnaire/ feedback form (paper)	The post-walkthrough questionnaire can address the following: • General impressions of the product based on the entire walkthrough • Specific questions that the team had about the tasks or particular interface features • Feedback about the pluralistic usability walkthrough procedure • General comments or possible design solutions.	Optional

(Continued)

Table 5.3 (Continued)		
Document or Item Name	**Description**	**Required or Optional**
Data summary forms (electronic)	Data summary forms are useful for collating the input from the problem reporting forms. In effect, the forms are a grid of participants, tasks, and steps in the task. The dependent measure is whether the participant described the correct action.	Optional

Planning a Pluralistic Usability Walkthrough Session

Follow these steps when planning a pluralistic usability walkthrough session:

1. **Decide whether the group walkthrough is the most appropriate evaluation method.** A review of the strengths and weaknesses shown earlier should help.
2. **Recruit a group of stakeholders that includes the following:**
   * An experienced facilitator (often the usability lead)
   * Four to ten actual or potential users or user surrogates (if users aren't available) who will role play the user's perspective
   * A few key developers
   * A usability practitioner
   * A product/project manager
   * A business analyst
   * A limited number of other internal stakeholders (QA, training, documentation, tech support).

   Because one goal is to have everyone voice an opinion, the size of the group should not get too large.

●●●

The success of a pluralistic usability walkthrough depends heavily on the skills of the facilitator in keeping the session collaborative rather than adversarial. The facilitator must ensure that users are not intimidated by the presence of developers and other members of the product team. The group dynamics of the pluralistic usability walkthrough should ideally generate empathy for the user during and after the session. Bias (1994) refers to this effect as "coordinated empathy." One theoretical benefit of coordinated empathy is that the empathy will persist and lead the product team to consider the impact of design decisions on users beyond a particular walkthrough.

3. **Choose a small set of tasks that are critical for product or feature success**. Lewis and Wharton (1997) note that the choice of tasks is a problem for any task-based evaluation method, especially ones such as cognitive and pluralistic usability walkthroughs that can only cover a very limited set of tasks. Common criteria for choosing tasks include the following:

   - **Absolutely required to access the product**. For example, logging into a system is an absolute requirement.
   - **Frequency**. Both high- and low-frequency tasks might be candidates. High-frequency tasks that have usability problems can affect morale and increase frustration for users and rapidly engender a bad reputation on social media. Low-frequency tasks, such as doing a database recovery after a power failure, may be done only a few times a year, but they may have a high criticality as explained in the next list item.
   - **Criticality**. Criticality can be viewed as the impact that the task has on the success or failure of a business or organization or some hazard to particular groups. In the design of medical devices that deliver drugs to patients automatically, the task of setting a dosage is of high criticality. Failure to set the proper dose could lead to patient harm and civil litigation.
   - **The level of concern that the product team has about the task**. Does the product team worry about the impact of the proposed UI on particular tasks? If your writers, quality engineers, or others have concern about a task, you might want to get user feedback to assuage (or intensify!) their fears.
   - **The importance of the task for generating a good first impression**. For some products, it is important for the first task to be simple and provide some immediate benefits to the user.
   - **Generality (the task is common across the interface so evaluating it has a high ROI)**. For example, if you use the same search interface in multiple places in your product, the feedback from the walkthrough can be generalized to other instances of search.
   - **Impact of change**. The interface for an important task has changed, and you want to know how difficult it is for established users to make the transition.

   Wharton and colleagues (1992, p. 387) made some specific recommendations regarding tasks for the cognitive walkthrough method that are also relevant for pluralistic usability walkthroughs:

- **Start with a simple task and move to more complex tasks**. This allows the participants to become familiar with the method and get a sense of expectations about how much detail, how the discussion will go, and so on.
- **Consider how many tasks you can complete in a single walkthrough session**. A common theme in the research and case study literature is that only a few tasks can be examined in any walkthrough session. A recommendation is to consider evaluating two to five tasks in any given session depending on task complexity.
- **Choose realistic tasks that include core features of the product**. Core features form the underpinning of a product. For example, core features in presentation software are "slides" that allow users to mix images, sound, graphics, and text; animation to enliven a slide; and templates that allow users to make custom layouts.
- **Consider tasks that involve multiple core features so you can get input on transitions among the core features**. For example in Microsoft Word, you might want to test the transition between basic editing and graphics features—two core features that are used in making business reports.
- **Consider tasks that use new high-priority features**. These are the tasks that are considered high priority by the marketing and product development teams (the "killer" feature that will "destroy" the competition!).

4. **The pluralistic usability walkthrough procedure requires a "correct path," so the facilitator of the walkthrough must decide which path is most appropriate (Bias, 1994) for each task**. If you suspect that there is another likely alternate path, you can review it after the primary path is reviewed.

5. **Prepare a document containing a set of screenshots that lead a participant through the path needed to complete a task**. The screenshots can include the following:
   - Entire screens, windows, and web pages
   - Dialog boxes and pop-up windows
   - Status and error messages
   - Detailed shots of particular interfaces (e.g., the results list from a web page).

   Table 5.4 is a simple example of the documentation required for a pluralistic usability walkthrough.

Table 5.4 Sample Screens and Pluralistic Usability Walkthrough Questions

Background: You are a member of a walkthrough team that will evaluate an interface for sending flowers to a family member.

Task: Send flowers for your mom for Mother's Day and include a note. She likes roses and lives 500 miles away.

SCREEN 1: Given the task, what would you do on this screen to get to the next screen? Please write your answer on the page.	SCREEN 2: Given the task, what would you do on this screen to get to the next screen? Please write your answer on the page.
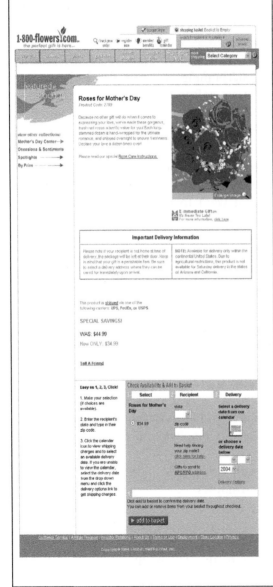	

SCREEN 3: Given the task, what would you do on this screen to get to the next screen? Please write your answer on the page.

SCREEN 4: Given the task, what would you do on this screen to get you to the next screen? Please write your answer on the page.

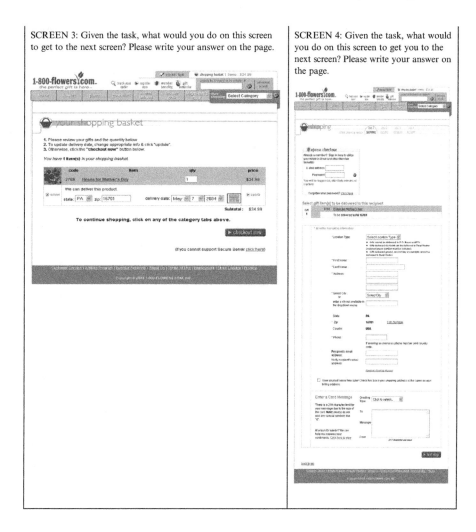

6. **If users are involved, the developers and other internal members of the walkthrough team need to be briefed on how to interact with users.**

Conducting a Pluralistic Usability Walkthrough Session

To conduct a pluralistic usability walkthrough session, follow these steps:

1. **When the evaluation team meets, have everyone introduce themselves.** Briefly discuss the goals and timeline for the walkthrough and then go over the basic instructions and ground rules. Provide an example of what you expect. The facilitator should indicate that he or she

may curtail discussion to ensure that the group gets through an adequate amount of material.

2. **Provide a brief overview of the product and key concepts**. This is usually done by a product expert. This should be a high-level overview and not deal with the specific tasks that the team will cover.

3. **Hand out the package of screens or web pages to the walkthrough team**. Consider having members of the team initial the package so you know the perspective of the person who marks up the screens (unless this violates the privacy of the individuals).

4. **Present the walkthrough team with the first task and image of the UI**.

5. **Ask each team member to write down what actions he or she would take to accomplish the task with the image that the team is looking at**. Each person does this individually without discussion. Table 5.5 shows an example using a museum website.

6. **After each person has written down his or her answer without discussion, the facilitator announces the correct answer, and the team discusses the results with users going first, followed by the human factors or usability participants, developers, and then the rest of the team**. This discussion focuses on potential usability problems. During this discussion, possible solutions to problems may be voiced, but this is not the place for extended discussions of solutions. Note any suggestions, but keep the focus on problems.

7. **When the team has gone through the entire task scenario represented by the screenshots, you can hold a brief general summary discussion (keep this short, or the group might lose its momentum)**.

8. **Introduce a new task scenario and new set of screenshots and go through each screen as before with the following instruction: "Given the task, what would you do on this screen to get you to the next screen? Please write your answer on the page."** Repeat steps 4 through 8 until you have gone through all of the tasks (or run out of time).

After the Pluralistic Usability Walkthrough Session

After the session, follow these steps:

1. **At the end of the walkthrough session, the packages of screenshots with comments are collected from all participants**. If you had a note-taker to take notes, those notes are collected and identified with some type of code.

Table 5.5 Example of a Page for the User to Mark with the Answer That Would Allow Completion of the Task

Background: You are a member of a walkthrough team that will evaluate the website of the DeCordova Museum.

Task: Find out how to drive to the DeCordova museum from the Massachusetts turnpike.

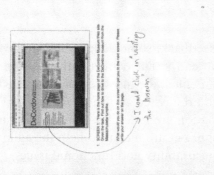

SCREEN 1: Here is the home page of the DeCordova Museum website. Given the task, what would you do on this screen to complete the task? Please write your answer on the page.

2. **Ask participants to fill out a short questionnaire about the overall usability of the product that they evaluated plus some specific questions that the product team was especially interested in**.
3. **Summarize the descriptions of what actions users would take at each step from the handouts and the group discussion and with any design solutions that emerge**.
4. **Catalog, prioritize, and assign problems, themes, and issues to the appropriate members of the product**. Arrange subsequent meetings to review solutions for the important problems.

VARIATIONS AND EXTENSIONS TO THE PLURALISTIC USABILITY WALKTHROUGH METHOD

This section describes variations and extensions of the pluralistic usability walkthrough method from the research and practitioner literature.

Agile Product Demos

To get continuous user feedback, some agile teams are inviting a small group of customers to attend sprint demos with the entire agile team available. In the product demos, the most recent completed user stories are demoed to users who are invited to provide feedback. The product demos with user participation are much less controlled than the pluralistic usability walkthrough, but are meant to help the agile team understand user concerns about usability and functional issues.

Remote Pluralistic Usability Walkthroughs

Pluralistic usability walkthroughs can be conducted remotely by using a mixture of video, audio, and remote collaboration software that allow group discussion, facial shots, and the display of screen images or prototypes to be seen at all locations. However, given the importance of face-to-face collaboration and discussion at each step in a task, remote pluralistic usability walkthroughs may be difficult. There may be situations where some observers may want to view the session (e.g., part of the development team at another site) and even follow along making their own comments about each step in a task but not engage in the discussion because it would slow the process down.

Collaborative Usability Inspection

Constantine and Lockwood (1999) describe a method called "collaborative usability inspection" that melds the pluralistic usability walkthrough

and heuristic evaluation methods. The focus of the collaborative usability inspection is on rapid identification of usability defects. Like the pluralistic review, Constantine and Lockwood ask the inspection team to put themselves in the role of user by cultivating a "practiced naiveté" (Constantine & Lockwood, 1999, p. 404). The participants in the inspection include a lead reviewer, a notetaker, developers, users, domain experts, usability specialists, and an optional "continuity expert" who focuses on consistency issues. The collaborative usability inspection has two phases: interactive inspection and static inspection.

In the interactive inspection phase, the participants walk through the scenarios using a prototype or actual product. Defects are noted by the recorder. Users are given priority in the discussion, but developers are urged to be active as well. At the end of each task scenario, the lead reviewer asks for general comments. Constantine and Lockwood make an important point that in addition to defects, good points about the design should be noted so these good points are not eliminated as development goes forward.

In the static inspection phase, the team explores different paths through the interface and examines various UI components (important web pages, dialog boxes or pop-up windows, icons, menus, overall layout, messages, error prevention) that may not have been covered in the interactive phase. The static phase focuses on breadth.

The length of collaborative usability inspections will vary by the scope and complexity of the product. For large and complex inspections, multiple sessions may be needed to prevent reviewer burnout.

Constantine and Lockwood propose that the lead reviewer have the final task of assembling the results of the inspection, prioritizing the defects, suggesting solutions, estimating the time for redesign, and assigning the redesigns to the product team. There are few usability practitioners who have enough clout to assign defects to a development team, so realistically, the lead reviewer would work with the development and product managers who determine what is fixed and when it will be fixed.

Details of the collaborative usability inspections can be found in the following resources: Constantine (1994) and Constantine and Lockwood (1999).

MAJOR ISSUES IN THE USE OF THE PLURALISTIC USABILITY WALKTHROUGH METHOD

Major issues that will face practitioners using the pluralistic usability walkthrough method are described in the section below.

Fixed Path for Tasks

The pluralistic usability walkthrough requires a complete set of screenshots or storyboards. Bias (1994) notes that every participant in the method must have a copy of the screenshots that would be seen by the users for a specified task. You can't do everything with paper that you can with working code. One limitation of this method is that it requires a specific task sequence so users cannot engage in unguided exploration or browsing as they often do with working products.

Narrow Focus

The pluralistic usability walkthrough has a relatively narrow focus compared to the heuristic evaluation, for example. You only get information on the particular path that is chosen by the walkthrough facilitator. If a participant chooses the incorrect path on a page, the reason for the choice is discussed, but then the participant and group must "reset" to the correct path and move on to the next step in the scenario. Care must be taken to ensure that participants who take a path other than the correct one are not made to feel like they made an error.

Requires a Strong Facilitator to Control the Discussion between Users and Team Members

The pluralistic usability walkthrough method requires a strong facilitator because of the potential for tension between developers and users (and other stakeholders as well) (Usability Body of Knowledge, n.d). Users might feel awkward critiquing the work of the developers in the session, and developers may react negatively to comments about their work. Prior to and during walkthroughs involving developers and users, this author has found that some coaching about how to interact with users and listen carefully can make quite a difference in the product team's reaction to the walkthrough and willingness to do it again. This coaching involves the following specific issues:

- Listening before reacting.
- Body language.
- Empathy for the user.

- Ideas about solutions, but no final decisions in the meeting.
- Early feedback to save time in the long run.

DATA, ANALYSIS, AND REPORTING

The primary data from a pluralistic review are the following:

- Choices about what each team member would do that are written on each screen in a scenario.
- Issues and problems that emerge during the group discussion.
- Design ideas for improving the UI that emerge during the group discussion.
- Number of users and other participants who choose the "correct action" on a screen.
- Post-walkthrough questionnaire.

These responses to each task scenario can be analyzed for the type, number, and severity of problems. The data from post-scenario surveys can provide ratings of difficulty. The questions that are asked during the walkthrough can also be analyzed for common themes. The suggestions for redesigns can be rated by relevant criteria such as feasibility, usability, and consistency.

CONCLUSIONS

The pluralistic usability walkthrough is a straightforward and participatory method designed to generate empathy for users. Facilitators guide users and members of the product team through a series of tasks and ask the users to mark screenshots with notes that indicate what they would do to complete a task. After the user writes his/her answer, the facilitator provides the "correct" answer. The user then discusses any usability issues followed by feedback from members of the product team. After each task, the users are asked to fill out a brief usability questionnaire. The method is powerful but probably best suited for more complex systems because of the costs and time involved.

Formal Usability Inspections

Alternate Names: Peer reviews, structured walkthroughs, inspections.

Related Methods: Heuristic evaluation, cognitive walkthrough, perspective-based inspections, pluralistic walkthrough.

OVERVIEW OF FORMAL USABILITY INSPECTIONS

The formal usability inspection method is derived from formal software inspections (Kahn & Prail, 1994). Formal usability inspections have a clearly defined process with trained inspectors, explicit roles for members of the inspection team, and a set of defined activities that generally include the following (Kahn & Prail, 1994; Wiegers, 2002):

1. **Planning** for the inspection and follow-up.
2. **A kickoff meeting** where the members of the team are introduced, given an overview, and trained in the basic usability inspection procedures. The moderator hands out the "inspection kit," which contains all of the materials necessary for the inspection.
3. **Individual preparation** by each member of the inspection team. During this stage of the process, each inspector conducts an independent review of a specific deliverable, which is included in the inspection kit. The inspectors are given some guidance on how to review the deliverable. In the classic article on this method (Kahn & Prail, 1994), inspectors were given user profiles, task scenarios, user and task heuristics, and a task performance model to guide the product review. Each inspector independently fills out a standard defect log that describes usability or design defects, where the defects are located, and other information.
4. **A group inspection meeting** where all the inspectors convene to list the defects they found as well as any new defects that emerge from the interaction of the inspectors.
5. **An explicit rework meeting** or document that commits to particular changes and solutions.
6. **Verification** of fixes and follow-up.

While other inspection methods, such as heuristic evaluations and cognitive walkthroughs, use some of the same activities, the difference here is the level of formality of the process and the use of the usability defect data to establish a historical database that can be used to track trends and usability defects, estimate ROI, and perhaps establish some level of statistical process control that can help eliminate major usability bugs.

Formal inspections can be conducted on many work products, including the following (IEEE, 2008; Kahn & Prail, 1994; Wiegers, 2002):

- Working products
- Requirements documents
- Business plans
- Functional specifications
- UI specifications
- Paper, medium fidelity, and working prototypes
- Style guides
- Software or UI architecture documents
- Workflow diagrams
- UI designs
- Online and hardcopy documentation.

Formal code inspections have a long history of providing a positive and cost-effective impact on software quality. Boehm and Basili (2001) report that inspections detect from 31% to 93% of defects with a median value of approximately 60%. Wiegers (2002) provides examples of the positive ROI for a variety of software projects. Similar values are not yet available for formal usability inspections because of a lack of published data. Early anecdotal data are positive (Gunn, 1995; Kahn & Prail, 1994), but to date, there is little direct empirical evidence of the benefits of formal usability inspections.

WHEN SHOULD YOU USE FORMAL USABILITY INSPECTIONS?

Formal usability inspections can be conducted throughout the development cycle though they are most useful during the early and middle phases of development for keeping usability bugs out of working code and minimizing rework (Table 6.1).

Table 6.2 illustrates the relative effort required, on average, to develop and use formal usability inspections.

STRENGTHS

Formal inspections have the following strengths:

- The method is based on code inspections. Many companies already use or are at least aware of code inspections in other areas, so the

Table 6.1 Phases of Development When Formal Usability Inspections Are Useful				
		✓	✓	✓
Problem Definition	Requirements	Conceptual Design	Detailed Design	Implementation

Table 6.2 Relative Effort and Resources Required for Formal Usability Inspection Development and Use				
Overall Effort Required	Time for Planning and Conducting	Skill and Experience	Supplies and Equipment	Time for Data Analysis
▣▣▣▣□	▣▣▣▣□	▣▣▣▣▣	▣▣▣□□	▣▣▣▣▣

method can be integrated into the overall development process as an existing method applied to the UI rather than "one of those new usability procedures." Inspections that start early (with requirements documents, specifications, and prototypes) can reduce usability defects before they become embedded in code.

- Formal usability inspections generally don't involve users, but the inclusion of user profiles, task scenarios, and guidelines on addressing problems from the perspective of a user makes this a much more user-centered process than simple screen-by-screen or page-by-page reviews (with no task orientation).

- The formal usability inspection method is useful for training inspectors about usability issues. The participants in the inspection will learn about usability issues and UI design principles and use that knowledge in future products (Gunn, 1995), with or without a UCD practitioner. In formal inspections that this author has conducted, inspectors were recruited from groups working on related products, or different areas of a large website, so they take what they learned back to their colleagues. You might call this "viral UCD" to borrow from the Internet advertising world.

- The formal inspection process involves a discussion of solutions and tracking of what problems get fixed and how. The tracking of fixes provides a measure of the method's impact. The formal inspection method also includes process improvement as part of the basic procedure.

- With remote conferencing tools, formal usability inspections can be conducted remotely.

WEAKNESSES

Formal inspections have the following weaknesses:

- Formal inspections are generally not suited for agile development.
- Formal usability inspections were given good press with the 1994 article by Kahn and Prail, but there have been few detailed case studies or research articles that validated or extended that early work.
- Formal inspections require a significant commitment of time for four to ten people.
- Some of the people who are key inspectors are often on the critical path for products and may be hard to recruit.
- Formal inspections can be viewed as threatening to the people whose products and deliverables are the object of inspections. Some members of a product team may fear that a long list of defects related to their product may not be good for job security.
- Getting everyone to prepare effectively can be difficult. The literature on formal code inspections tends to take a hard line on individual preparation. Some books consider asking anyone who is not prepared to leave the inspection meeting. The value of this method largely depends on the quality of the individual reviews, so moderators need to make this point clearly. One small tip here is to send a reminder several days early (three to four days seems to work best) with a minor statement that is designed to invoke a bit of guilt for coming to the group inspection meeting unprepared.
- On complex products, you can only inspect a portion of the UI, so it can be challenging to decide what to inspect. Freedman and Weinberg (1990) note that sampling is risky because one major error can be catastrophic. They relate a story about an Australian firm that missed a defect because it only sampled a requirements document for review. The estimated cost of the missed defect was $250,000,000.

WHAT DO YOU NEED TO USE THE FORMAL USABILITY INSPECTION?

This section provides a brief description of the basic resources needed to conduct a formal usability inspection.

Personnel, Participants, and Training

A formal usability inspection generally involves participants with the following roles (IEEE, 2008; Kahn & Prail, 1994; Wiegers, 2002):

- **Moderator**. Also called the inspection leader, facilitator, lead reviewer, and review leader depending on the reference, this person is responsible for all the management and administrative functions, such as choosing an inspection team, compiling the documents needed for the inspection, defining the objectives (with the author), running the inspection meeting, compiling the data, and making process improvements that will benefit future inspections. There is one moderator for each inspection. The moderator can also serve in the role of inspector.
- **Author (owner, lead designer/developer)**. The author is the person responsible for a deliverable. In the inspection literature, there is a debate about how active an author can be during an inspection (Wiegers, 2002). The general rule is that an author cannot be a moderator, reader, or notetaker because he or she cannot be objective. Wiegers suggests that having the author as an inspector can be useful because the discussions might trigger the author to note defects that others may not because of familiarity with the product.
- **Recorder (notetaker)**. The recorder documents all of the defects that emerge from a formal inspection and records all action items, decisions, and recommendations. The recorder also records any suggestions for improving the inspection process. When resources are limited, the moderator can act as a recorder, but that can be difficult, especially when formal usability inspections are introduced into a development environment. Kahn and Prail (1994) suggest that the recording responsibilities can be dedicated to inspectors or rotated among inspectors, but this introduces variability in the recording skills and is not recommended. Choose someone who is very good at capturing defects and issues, and avoid rotating the duty among inspectors. Other requirements for the role of recorder include (Freedman & Weinberg, 1990) the following:
  - An understanding of the vocabulary used in the deliverables.
  - Objectivity in taking notes. Recorders should be cautious about editorial comments.
  - Accuracy in recording defects and issues.
  - Sufficient background to understand the issues.
  - Time to write up the results after an inspection.

- Dedication to following up on the distribution of reports, the compilation of reviews, and the archiving of the final report so it is accessible later.
- **Inspectors.** The inspectors are recruited to find and report on defects and to contribute to design solutions. The inspection team generally consists of four to eight people. Criteria for the choice of inspectors can vary depending on the deliverable and product, but you may want to include colleagues who have the following traits:
  - Knowledgeable about the product but not directly involved with the deliverable being inspected
  - Significant domain and/or usability knowledge
  - Not under the management of the product being reviewed
  - Known to be quality reviewers (based on previous experience)
  - Knowledgeable of users and how they might interact with the product
  - Some outsiders (possibly users who are known to technical support).

  Managers are often not invited to inspections because of the tendency to evaluate the author and other members of the inspection team. Wiegers (2002) notes that inspectors (especially the author of the product) may feel like the exposure of defects in a deliverable will be counted against them during performance evaluation, which goes counter to the philosophy that exposing defects is a good thing and not an indicator of professional incompetence. Inviting managers might depend on the general relationship between the manager and the inspection team. If there is an excellent relationship, and the manager doesn't run his or her team by fear, it might be acceptable to have the manager present, although the moderator should strongly consider some coaching about appropriate (non-threatening) behavior.
- **Reader (optional).** The role of the reader is to present the material being inspected in small bits to the inspection team. The reader describes the material in his or her own words. The assumption here is that having a reader interpret the deliverable may reveal defects or stimulate discussion about the material. This is similar to having respondents read questionnaires out loud as part of pilot testing. The act of reading aloud often prompts questions or comments from the questionnaire participant. The role of reader might be most appropriate for documents such as UI specification, requirements, style guides, or functional specifications.

- **Observers.** Observers are people who do not actively contribute to the goals of the inspection. Keep the number of observers small and make sure that the observers are clear on the ground rules and their role. There may be strong pressure to have many observers when you are starting your inspections.
- **Standards bearer (optional).** A standards bearer is responsible for ensuring that any standards, patterns, or guidelines that relate to usability or the UI are followed. This person may also focus on the general area of consistency. This is a particular perspective that could be part of any formal review (see Chapter 3 on perspective-based inspections).

Hardware and Software

If you have a working product or prototype, you need to provide the inspectors with all of the requisite hardware and software and also the list of requirements for running the software (memory, browser, special equipment, disk space, etc.).

Although it isn't absolutely necessary, a method for projecting the defects and issues is recommended so the entire inspection team can see what is being recorded. If no projection system is available, then defects can be listed on flip charts or sticky notes. Some type of archive is useful for examining defects across projects and tracking the impact of the formal inspections. The archive can be the corporate bug database, an Excel spreadsheet, or a separate database.

Documents and Materials

The inspection packet contains most of the documents that are required for a formal usability inspection. Here are the most important documents:

- **Inspection instructions (these will vary depending on whether you are evaluating documents, prototypes, storyboards, etc.).**
- **A profile of the users or personas that are important for the deliverable you are reviewing.**
- **Descriptions of the context and tasks descriptions or scenarios.** The level of detail of these descriptions will vary with the particular deliverable being inspected. One caution on the use of task scenarios is that the level of detail you provide may affect the number of problems you find. For example, if your tasks scenarios are too specific

and point people to specific menu items, this might yield fewer problems than if you used a more abstract scenario. This level of task abstraction will vary with the type of deliverable you are inspecting (paper prototype versus beta version of a product).

- **Inspection aids such as checklists or a list of heuristics that are specific to the deliverable.** Kahn & Prail (1994), for example, used a mixture of task-based and user-based heuristics from Shneiderman (1987), Nielsen and Molich (1990), and other UCD sources. If you were inspecting a user's guide, you might use documentation heuristics (Purho, 2000).
- **Product and/or feature descriptions that provide a general overview of the product or features that you will be inspecting.**
- **Supporting documents.** For example, if you are reviewing a working prototype, you may also want to review the draft documentation. Common supporting documents include UI style guides (violations of the style guide are considered defects), branding guides, or functional specifications.
- **A list of inspection team members, a schedule, and a location for the meeting.**
- **Usability defect form.** This form is used during the preparation phase of the inspection when the inspectors work alone.
- **A list of known defects or limitations.** This list alerts inspectors about usability defects that they do *not* have to spend time on during the inspection.
- **Other relevant supporting materials.**

PROCEDURES AND PRACTICAL ADVICE ON FORMAL USABILITY INSPECTIONS

This section describes how to plan and conduct a formal usability inspection.

Deciding When to Hold Formal Usability Inspections

Formal inspections are generally part of the overall development schedule and are often used for authorizing a deliverable if it demonstrates the required level of quality in the inspection, to move to the next stage of development. In the usability inspection context, you may want to define the formal inspection checkpoints in the project schedule but be open to formal or informal usability inspections if design issues come up or developers/designers ask for assistance between formal reviews. A formal inspection is sometimes planned as part of a comprehensive release readiness review.

Choosing a Moderator

General qualities of a good moderator are discussed later in this chapter, but here are some of the attributes of a good moderator for a usability inspection:

- Training in general facilitation techniques
- General background in usability and UI design principles
- Familiarity with the inspection process (if your company has a formal code inspection process, adapting it for usability might make usability inspections more acceptable to management)
- Impartiality
- Reasonable technical and domain knowledge beyond usability
- The strength to keep inspections on track and to "enforce" the formal inspections rules
- Respect from the members of the inspection team.

Some companies have professional moderators who might be able to help, but they may not have sufficient background in usability or the time to follow up and see what solutions were implemented.

Planning

Formal planning begins when an "author" of a deliverable has a document, prototype, or other work product ready for review. The author might be a UCD practitioner who wants to have a UI specification reviewed, a development manager who wants a product requirement or functional specification document reviewed, or a UI designer who has a workflow diagram or prototype. The author has ownership of the deliverable that is to be inspected.

A successful UI inspection begins with a formal plan that is created jointly by the moderator and author. The formal inspection plan includes the following steps (Kahn & Prail, 1994):

1. Define the goals of the formal usability inspection.
2. Describe what deliverables will be inspected and how much can be accomplished. This is critical because a formal inspection cannot cover all of the interface components of any complex product, or an entire user's guide, or the seventy-five wireframes that the

creative team came up with. Consider establishing criteria for deciding what aspects of the deliverable are most critical. Here are several criteria, but you may need to consider others depending on the schedule, time, importance of the product, and so on:

- Product definition deliverables. The early documents are critical because there is much evidence that poor requirements or early specifications can create the need for a significant rework later.
- New features or interface components that are being touted as a critical competitive advantage.
- Features that will have high usage.
- Features that are part of mission-critical tasks (things that can cause severe safety or economic risk).

●●●————————————————————————————————

Entry Criteria for Usability Inspections

The moderator of the inspection is responsible for reviewing the inspection deliverable and determining if the deliverable is of sufficient quality (Wiegers, 2002). There is a trade-off to consider with respect to the deliverable that will be inspected: if the deliverable (e.g., UI specification) is very rough and not yet stable, you may need to conduct multiple formal inspections, which can be excessively resource intensive.

In the case of an early deliverable, consider using informal review methods such as heuristic evaluations until the deliverable becomes more stable, and then conduct the formal inspection. Another entry criterion is that the members of the inspection team have at least basic training in the procedures before the group inspection meeting.

——

3. Choose the inspection team. Some detailed criteria for team roles are discussed later in this chapter.
4. Create the inspection packet. The inspection packet will vary with the deliverable, but common contents of this package include the following:
   - Inspection instructions (these will vary depending on whether you are evaluating documents, prototypes, storyboards, etc.).
   - A "typos list" for very minor spelling, grammar, or cosmetic problems. This list is filled out during the individual inspection and just handed in during the group meeting. The author uses the typos lists to fix minor problems. Figure 6.1 shows a typos list adapted from Wiegers (2002, p. 85).
   Minor typos are not mentioned during the formal inspection to save time, but are captured so they can be corrected. The

---

Usability Inspection Typos List

Instructions: Record any minor typographic errors that you find during your review of the usability inspection deliverable, including any spelling, grammar, formatting, and style errors. These are errors that should be corrected but do not have to be discussed during the inspection meeting. If you feel that a typo or other error will have a major impact on the product (for example, you discover that a missing word in an instruction may result in lost data), then that error should be expressed at the meeting. The minor typos on this list will not be counted as usability defects.

Product Being Inspected: _____

Location of Problem   Description of Typo
_____   _____

Figure 6.1 Template for a typos list.

rationale for a separate typos list that is compiled only during the individual review is that it can save time during the inspection meeting. On a psychological note, it also removes a criticism that UI reviews sometimes get bogged down with trivial things such as typos.

Typos Can Be Critical!

There is another side to the question about typos. Wiegers (2002) notes that a typo in a requirements document can change the requirement considerably and be a serious defect (e.g., if you had a product that was supposed to monitor events down to "1/1000 of a second," but your spec reads "1/10 of a second," that difference might be catastrophic if you were developing a system for a jet airliner). Similarly, a misspelling of the company name in the home page of a website prototype is a typo but also a defect which may have legal consequences. So, while it might be worth having a typos list to keep the group inspection meeting from bogging down, be sure not to dismiss all typos as minor.

- A profile of the users or a description of the primary or secondary personas.
- Inspection aids such as checklists or a list of heuristics that are specific to the deliverable. These should be tailored to the particular deliverable and not be too lengthy because it is hard to keep long checklists or many heuristics in mind.

Table 6.3 A Simple Defect Logging Template for Individual Inspectors			
Inspection Date:			
Inspector Name:			
Location of Defect	**Description**	**Category [Optional]**	**Severity [Optional]**
[Task, screen, page, or other location information]	[Succinct description that will be understood several weeks after the meeting.]		

- Descriptions of the context and tasks descriptions or scenarios. The level of detail of these descriptions will vary with the particular deliverable being inspected.
- Product and/or feature descriptions that provide a general overview of the product or features that you will inspecting.
- Supporting documents. For example, if you are reviewing a working prototype, you may also want to review the draft documentation. Common supporting documents include UI style guides (violations of the style guide are considered defects), branding guides, or functional specifications.
- A list of inspection team members, a schedule, and a location for the meeting.
- Usability defect logging form. This form is used during the preparation phase of the inspection when the inspectors work alone. The form can be paper or electronic. This form should be simple and used by the recorder as well as the inspectors. Table 6.3 gives a simple defect logging template.
- A list of known defects or limitations. This list alerts inspectors about usability defects that they do *not* have to spend time on during the inspection.
- Other relevant supporting materials.

Kickoff Meeting

The kickoff meeting can be held as soon as the inspection packet is ready. The goals of the kickoff meeting are to do the following:

- Introduce the team members to one another.
- Distribute the inspection packets and review the contents.
- Review the procedures for the inspection and conduct training on the inspection process.

- Have the author provide a general description of the product or component, including a demonstration and information on how to gain access to any materials or prototypes on the web.
- Distribute passwords if required.
- Remind the inspection team of the schedule and their individual obligations.
- Create a shared vision of the process and its outcomes.

Kickoff meetings should have a clear agenda and be relatively brief (thirty to sixty minutes). At the meeting, the inspectors are invited to contact the moderator or author if they have any procedural or technical questions about the inspection process or the deliverable that is being inspected. If there are observers or managers who are interested in the procedures, they can be invited to the kickoff meeting rather than the group inspection meeting.

Individual Preparation

During the preparation phase, the inspectors work alone. Their task is to review the entire deliverable and materials in the inspection packet and then record usability defects and issues. In formal usability inspections, the team members are generally asked to take the role of users as defined in the user profile. Alternatively, inspectors might be asked to take different perspectives (Basili, Green, Shull, Sorumgaard, & Zelkowitz 1996; also see Chapter 2, Perspective-Based Inspections, in this handbook).

Inspectors use a defect reporting form to log all defects and issues that emerge during their individual reviews. The inspectors generally log the following (Kahn & Prail, 1994):

- Where the defect was found.
- A description of the defect that will be generally understood.
- A classification of the problem (optional). The categories can vary with the deliverable, and if you do ask inspectors to classify problems, the scheme should be reasonably simple and be in the inspection packet.
- Ideas for solutions (optional). This is sometimes not included on defect forms, but jotting down an idea for a solution may be helpful later. Inspectors should be forewarned not to spend much time on this because the purpose of the inspection is to detect defects; any "solutions" are just quick entries to aid recall. If your inspector spends time

drawing a new screen layout to fix a workflow problem, he or she is likely to miss many defects, and, in the end, other issues may make the proposed screen layout worthless, so much time will be wasted.

- Severity ratings. This could be very simple—major/minor—or you can follow a more detailed defect severity scale. If severity ratings are expected during the individual preparation, the definitions of severity should be explained in the kickoff meeting. There is a long history in UCD of inconsistency in severity ratings. The structure and training of the formal usability inspection is intended to improve the consistency of assigning severities, but there is little data on whether severity ratings become more consistent when teams are trained in defect definitions and given some practice before assigning severity levels to actual usability defects.

The Inspection Meeting

After the inspectors have conducted their individual reviews of the deliverable, they meet to compile their defects and find additional defects. At this meeting, the moderator or reader walks through scenarios, flows, screens, or documents, and then poses questions to the group. The inspectors report all defects that they found during the individual preparation and any new defects that are found as a result of the group interaction. The moderator's goal here is to keep the process efficient, cover the planned material without rushing at the end, and ensure that everyone understands all of the defects. If there is something that seems to cause problems (some claim it is a defect, but others see it as a feature—rare but does happen), the ambiguous issue can be recorded and discussed later.

●●●————————————————————————————————

What Happens If Your Inspectors Are Not Prepared?

The success of the inspection meeting is predicated on the individual preparation of team members. Some books on inspection procedures recommend that inspection meetings be postponed if the moderator feels that the group is not prepared. One set of rules suggested that the moderator "sends the unprepared person home" and continues with the remaining inspectors. Wiegers (2002) suggests a "study hall" approach where the inspectors meet after the kickoff meeting or a day or two before the group inspection meeting to review the deliverables. The IEEE standard for software reviews (IEEE, 2008) requires the following of the moderator:

"The inspection leader shall verify that inspectors are prepared for the inspection. The inspection leader shall reschedule the meeting if the inspectors are not adequately prepared. The inspection leader should gather individual preparation times and record the total in the inspection documentation."

The key issue here is that the moderator must persuade the team members that individual preparation is critical to the success of the usability inspection.

Inspectors point out usability defects and issues as the moderator or reader leads the groups through the scenarios or sections of the deliverable. The moderator can let the inspectors call out defects and issues or institute a round-robin procedure where each inspector is asked for his or her input until no one has any additional issues. Whatever procedure you use should be described in the kickoff meeting so no one is surprised.

During the inspection meeting, the recorder logs all defects, issues, and (briefly stated) solutions. Because inspections are meant to be public events, the recorder should use a projection device to display the defects to all participants. The moderator has to pace the session so the recorder can keep up with the defect rate. As a side note, the recorder should be a good typist and have enough background to log defects accurately. Having a person who is purely administrative with little product background may slow things down. Table 6.4 is a template for a simple logging form. Note that there is no record of who found defects because the goal of an inspection is to find defects, not rate the inspectors. The category and severity ratings can be deferred.

You generally want consensus on whether each defect is a "real" defect (this is probably more of an issue in usability inspections than in code inspections). You can ask inspectors to state when they think something is not a defect and ask the recorder to note that there is not a consensus among inspectors on that item. Do not get involved in discussion about the "realness" of a defect at this point. You can address that at the end of the meeting or at a separate meeting, update the inspection records, and let everyone know about the resolution of the defect disagreement.

The moderator should plan breaks, at least one every hour, and sessions should probably not last more than two to three hours on a given day because the inspection process is very demanding. Break the inspection into multiple meetings if you have a great deal to cover.

At the end of the meeting, it is often worthwhile to go through the list and ask for possible solutions and whether the problem is a major or minor defect. Each defect should be assigned to a specific responsible person (who might then delegate that out to others). If the defects were recorded online, the recorder should send the list out to all of the inspectors as well as other stakeholders, such as managers. Inspection results are generally public documents, so they should be placed where they can be retrieved by stakeholders who are not at the group meeting.

A final activity for the inspection process is a brief "process improvement" questionnaire. Inspectors can be invited to speak with the moderator privately in addition to providing process improvement data on the questionnaire.

Rework

During the rework phase of the usability inspection process, the author of the deliverable works with the moderator and design team on

Table 6.4 Template for a Defect Logging Form			
Project Name:			
Phase of Development Cycle:			
☐ Requirements ☐ Concept Development ☐ Design ☐ Detailed Design ☐ Implementation ☐ Testing, Release ☐ Post-release ☐ Maintenance			
Inspection Date:			
Moderator: **Recorder:**			
Total Number of Usability Defects Found: ___Major ____ Minor			
Total Number of Usability Defects Corrected: ___Major ____ Minor			
[The "defects corrected" fields are filled out when corrections are verified and used to determine the impact of the inspection—number of problems corrected/number of problems found. This defect log serves as an official record of the results.]			
Location of Defect	**Description**	**Category [Optional]**	**Severity**
[Task, screen, page, or other location information]	[Succinct description that will be understood several weeks after the meeting.]		

determining the best solution for each defect. The specific procedures here will vary with product complexity and the phase of the development cycle.

Follow-Up and Verification

The final step is to follow up with the author and others who are involved in making fixes and verify which defects have been fixed. Kahn and Prail (1994) suggest that teams examine the number of defects found by the total number of hours put in by the entire inspection team and also look at the ratio of defects found to defects fixed. The field on the defect log in Table 6.4 for "Total Number of Usability Problems Corrected" is filled in at this step in the inspection process.

All of the defects that are found through usability inspections should be aggregated in an inspection database or tagged so you know which defects emerged from your formal usability inspections. You can use this aggregated data to see if there are any patterns in the type or severity of defects.

MAJOR ISSUES WITH FORMAL USABILITY INSPECTIONS

Major issues that will face practitioners of formal usability inspections are described in the section below.

Should You Report Positive Findings?

Books and articles on usability often recommend that you report positive findings as well as usability defects. The philosophy of formal inspections is somewhat different because it has evolved as a formal defect detection system. Reporting positive findings is sometimes not recommended except in the case where fixing one defect might affect another important positive feature (Freedman & Weinberg, 1990). In this special case, you only report the positive finding because it interacts with a defect.

Constantine and Lockwood (1999) offer a different approach to positive findings. They note that it can be easier on developers and designers (who are often the "authors" in usability inspections) if some time is allocated to identifying positive features or aspects of the deliverable that contribute to a usable product. Constantine and Lockwood suggest that these positive aspects can be mentioned after the defects are identified (p. 404). One approach that you can take is to ask each inspector to list at least one positive aspect of the product that contributes to usability during the individual inspection and then raise that during the "positive findings" activity at the end of the group meeting.

Encourage Practiced Naiveté Among Inspectors

Constantine and Lockwood (1999) recommend that moderators encourage "practiced naiveté" where inspectors adopt the perspective of naive users who have never seen or used a product. This is an example of the perspective-based inspection approach (see Chapter 2). For this to be successful, the moderator needs to explain how to achieve a state of naiveté. Constantine and Lockwood also recommend that the inspectors work independently and do not ask anyone for help (although seeking clarification is okay).

Managers Must Be Supportive Without Being Invited

Formal inspection meetings should never be viewed as a way to evaluate the performance of the author of a deliverable or the inspectors. To reduce the chance that inspections are not performance appraisals, managers should generally not be invited (though if the manager is the author of the requirements or other deliverables, you might make an exception as long as the manager promises not to take out his or her anger on the inspectors who find defects in the manager's deliverable). Although managers may not be invited, the support of managers is critical (Freedman & Weinberg, 1990; Gunn, 1995; Kahn & Prail, 1994). Freedman and Weinberg (1990) offer some rules for managers:

- Include time in the project schedule for formal usability inspections.
- Encourage staff to prepare for inspections seriously and give them some time to do this.
- Reward good inspections of bad products.
- Do not use inspection reports as input into performance evaluations.

Defining "Problem" and "Issue"

The definition of "problem" is a controversial topic in UCD research and real-world contexts. In formal code inspections, the model on which formal usability inspections are based, the definition of what constitutes a "problem" and what constitutes an "issue" should be included in the training and the inspection. For example, "I don't like green" is a personal preference and most likely not a problem; "The green text on a red background is hard to read because of low contrast and chromostereopsis," is a problem. More problematic might be something that occurred because the person was evaluating a working prototype but was using the Mozilla Firefox browser, which wasn't on the approved browser list. The use of a different browser might be a quality or requirements issue but not technically a "usability problem," so this might be recorded as an "issue," or you might even have to disqualify feedback from the person not using an authorized browser if having a specific browser was a part of the formal evaluation instructions. The instructions and training for a formal usability evaluation should clearly define "problem" and "issue," and the moderator should be open to answering questions regarding this topic during the individual preparation phase.

DATA, ANALYSIS, AND REPORTING

The following basic types of data are collected during a formal usability inspection:

- The number and types of participants.
- The background of the participants. This can be useful in determining what mix of product, domain, and other experience constitutes an effectiveness team.
- The degree of coverage of the deliverable (number of screens, features, pages, help frames, etc.).
- The numbers of problems and issues.
- The location of problems and issues (what screen, what page, what screen object, what item in a list, etc.).
- The ratings or judgments of severity.
- The time spent on the various activities.
- Feedback on participants' perception of the effectiveness of the process.
- Various cross-tabulations of these basic types of data (e.g., "time spent in review by number of defects found").

These basic data can be grouped into several categories and combined to yield metrics that deal with effectiveness, efficiency, and satisfaction with the process. Table 6.5 (adapted from Wiegers, 2002, pp. 130–131) gives those categories, various metrics, and descriptions of each metric.

Table 6.5 Formal Inspection Metrics

Category	Name	Description
Amount of interface that is inspected	Planned amount of UI (metric depends on what is being inspected)	This is the number of screens, pages, windows, help files, and so on that you want to inspect.
	Actual amount of UI (metric depends on what is being inspected)	This is the actual number of screens, pages, windows, help files, and so on that you inspected.
Effort	Planning effort (person-hours)	The total number of person-hours spent planning the formal usability inspection. This is the sum of all of the time spent by team members.
	Overview and training effort (person-hours)	The total number of person-hours spent in the overview meeting and any additional training. This is the sum of all of the time spent by team members.
	Preparation effort (person-hours)	The total number of person-hours spent doing individual reviews of item being inspected. This is the sum of the time spent reviewing by all of the inspectors.
	Meeting effort (person-hours)	The total number of person-hours spent in inspection meetings, which is the number of people times the length of the meeting.
	Rework effort (person-hours)	This is the total person-hours spent correcting the defects based on the inspection results. This includes the time required to verify that the correction was a real solution and did not introduce the same or different problem. This can involve just a usability person or an entire development team depending on the severity and complexity of the defect.
Defects	Major defects found	The number of major defects found during an inspection that were judged as major.
	Minor defects found.	The number of minor defects found during an inspection that were judged as minor.
	Major defects corrected	The number of major defects that were corrected.
	Minor defects corrected	The number of minor defects that were corrected.
	Ratio of major/minor defects corrected to major/minor defects found	A measure of the effectiveness of the inspection.
	Defect density (number of defects found per unit of inspection material)	This is an indicator of the general quality of the item being inspected and also is used to determine the effectiveness of defect prevention when a product or feature is subject to multiple inspections (e.g., you inspect the UI specification and then the working prototype).
	Percent of errors that were major errors	This is the ratio of major defects found divided by the total number of defects times 100. This gives you a sense whether the inspection is finding major or minor problems.

(Continued)

Table 6.5 (Continued)		
Category	Name	Description
Other	Number of inspectors	The number of people who participated in the inspection meeting.
	Post-inspection appraisal	The inspection team's assessment of the product after the inspection: accepted as is—no major issues; accepted conditionally after major issues fixed, requires re-inspection after defects have been corrected; incomplete inspection.
	Inspection evaluation data	This is the feedback from the participants about the efficacy of the inspection process. This can be a combination of ratings scales and open-ended questions plus personal feedback.

Wiegers (2002) describes three types of analysis: effectiveness, efficiency, and ROI. While there are some data about these measures in the software engineering world, ROI for formal usability inspections has not been established. If you plan to use this method, you can begin with some of the simple measures in Table 6.5 and then consider some of the "justification" measures described here.

Effectiveness deals with the number of problems you find versus the total number of defects in a product. Because the purpose of formal usability inspections is to catch problems early so you don't have to spend more time and money later to fix defects, you might want to compare the number and types of problems that you found versus problems that slipped through the formal reviewed and showed up later in the development process. You might see that particular types of problems are not being identified because you are missing a key person on the inspection team or the scenarios you used are deficient in some way.

Efficiency deals with the number of defects you find per hour of effort. The goal of inspections is to minimize the average cost of finding a defect.

ROI has become a serious issue for UCD practitioners, especially for methods that don't fall under the "discount usability" umbrella (Bias & Mayhew, 2005). This topic is beyond the scope of this chapter, but Wiegers (2002) provides some general approaches for estimating the ROI of software inspections that can be applied to formal usability inspections. Tracking the effort for each step of the usability inspection process is a key part of the ROI analysis. To calculate ROI estimates, you need to know the hourly costs of finding, fixing, and validating the usability problems.

CONCLUSIONS

The formal usability inspection might seem like a dinosaur—large and out of place in this agile world. However, you can take portions of the procedures in this chapter and apply those portions that support goals like the collection of metrics to justify your work and tips like having a "standards" bearer who is a designated expert on standards, patterns, and guidelines. You might, for example, apply some of the formal procedures (e.g., listing known problems before the inspection beings so you don't waste time bringing them up again or providing a page for "typos") to the semi-formal group heuristic evaluation.

REFERENCES

Adlin, T., & Pruitt, J. (2010). *The essential persona lifecycle: Your guide to building and using personas.* San Francisco, CA: Morgan Kaufmann.

Akers, D., Jeffries, R., Simpson, M., & Winograd, T. (2012). Backtracking events as indicators of usability problems in creation-oriented applications. *ACM Transactions on Computer-Human Interaction, 19*(2) Article 16 (July 2012).

Bailey, R. (1999). Heuristic evaluation. *UI Design Newsletter—May, 1999.* Retrieved August 30, 2013, from <http://www.humanfactors.com/downloads/may99.asp>

Bailey, R. W., Allan, R. W., & Raiello, P. (1992). Usability testing vs. heuristic evaluation: A head-to-head comparison. In: *Proceedings of the 36th annual human factors society meeting* (pp. 409–413). Atlanta, GA.

Baker, K., Greenberg, S., & Gutwin, C. (2002). *Empirical development of a heuristic evaluation methodology for shared workspace groupware* (pp. 96–105). In: *Proceedings of the 2002 ACM conference on computer supported cooperative work (CSCW'02).* New York, NY: ACM.

Basili, V., Green, S., Laitenberger, O., Shull, F., Sorumgaard, S., & Zelkowitz, M. (1996). The empirical investigation of perspective-based reading. *Empirical Software Engineering: An International Journal, 1*(2), 133–164.

Bias, R. (1991). Interface—walkthroughs: Efficient collaborative testing. *IEEE Software, 8*(5), 58–59.

Bias, R. G. (1994). The pluralistic usability walkthrough: Coordinated empathies. In J. Nielsen, & R. Mack (Eds.), *Usability inspection methods* (pp. 63–76). New York, NY: John Wiley.

Bias, R. G., & Mayhew, D. J. (2005). *Cost-justifying usability: An update for the internet age* (2nd ed.). San Francisco, CA: Morgan Kaufmann.

Boehm, B., & Basili, V. (2001). Software defect reduction top 10 list. *IEEE Computer, 34*(1), 135–137.

Buley, L. (2013). *The user experience team of one: A research and design survival guide.* Brooklyn, NY: Rosenfeld Media.

Chattratichart, J., & Lindgaard, G. (2008). *A comparative evaluation of heuristic-based usability inspection methods* (pp. 2213–2220). CHI'08 extended abstracts on human factors in computing systems (*CHI EA'08*). New York, NY: ACM.

Chisnell, D., Redish, G., & Lee, A. (2006). *New heuristics for understanding older adults as web users.* Retrieved August 11, 2013, from <http://www.usabilityworks.net/resources/chisnell_redish_lee_heuristics.pdf>.

Cockton, G., Woolrych, A., Hornbæk, K., & Frøkjær, E. (2012). Inspection-based methods. In A. Sears, & J. A. Jacko (Eds.), *The human-computer interaction handbook: Fundamentals, evolving technologies and emerging applications* (3rd ed., pp. 1275–1293). Boca Raton, FL: CRC Press.

Constantine, L. L. (1994). Collaborative usability inspections for software. In: *Proceedings from software development '94.* San Francisco, CA: Miller Freeman.

Constantine, L. L., & Lockwood, L. A. (1999). *Software for use: A practical guide to the models and methods of usage centered design.* New York, NY: Addison-Wesley. (pp. 400).

Desurvire, H. (1994). *Faster, cheaper: Are usability inspection methods as effective as empirical testing?* New York, NY: John Wiley & Sons.

Desurvire, H., & Wiberg, C. (2008). *Master of the game: Assessing approachability in future game design* (pp. 3177–3182). CHI'08 extended abstracts on human factors in computing systems (*CHI EA'08*). New York, NY: ACM.

Doubleday, A., Ryan, M., Springett, M., & Sutcliffe, A. (1997). A comparison of usability techniques for evaluating design. In S. Coles (Ed.), In: *Proceedings of the second conference on designing interactive systems: Processes, practices, methods, and techniques (DIS'97)* (pp. 101–110). New York, NY: ACM.

Dumas, J., & Redish, J. (1999). *A practical guide to usability testing* (Revised ed.). Exeter, UK: Intellect.

FAA. (n.d.). *Formal usability evaluation.* Retrieved August 13, 2013, from <http://www.hf.faa.gov/workbenchtools/default.aspx?rPage = Tooldetails&subCatId = 13&toolID = 78>

Fagan, M. (1976). Design and code inspections to reduce errors in program development. *IBM Systems Journal, 15*(3), 182–211.

Freedman, D. P., & Weinberg, G. W. (1990). *Handbook of walkthroughs, inspections, and technical reviews: Evaluating programs, projects, and products* (3rd ed.). New York, NY: Dorset House Publishing.

Gerhardt-Powals, J. (1996). Cognitive engineering principles for enhancing human-computer performance. *International Journal of Human-Computer Interaction, 8*(2), 189–221.

Gilb, T., & Graham, D. (1993). *Software inspection.* London: Addison-Wesley Longman.

Grigoreanu, V., & Mohanna, M. (2013). *Informal cognitive walkthroughs (ICW): Paring down and pairing up for an agile world* (pp. 3093–3096). In: *Proceedings of the 2013 ACM annual conference: Human factors in computing systems (CHI'13).* New York, NY: ACM Press.

Grossman, T., Fitzmaurice, G., & Attar, R. (2009). *A survey of software learnability: Metrics, methodologies and guidelines* (pp. 649–658). In: *Proceedings of the SIGCHI conference on human factors in computing systems (CHI'09).* New York, NY: ACM.

Grudin, J. (1989). The case against user interface consistency. *Communications of the ACM, 32*(10), 1164–1173.

Gunn, C. (1995). An example of formal usability inspections in practice at Hewlett-Packard company. In: *Proceeding of the conference on human factors in computing system (CHI'95)* (pp. 103–104). Denver, CO, May 7–11, 1995.

Hartson, H. R., Andre, T. S., & Williges, R. C. (2003). Criteria for evaluating usability evaluation methods. *International Journal of Human-Computer Interaction, 15*(1), 145–181.

Hartson, R., & Pyla, P. (2012). *The UX book: Process and guidelines for ensuring a quality user interface.* Waltham, MA: Morgan Kaufmann.

Hertzum, M., & Jacobsen, N. E. (2001). The evaluator effect: A chilling fact about usability evaluation methods. *International Journal of Human-Computer Interaction, 13*(4).

Hertzum, M., Jacobsen, N. E., & Molich, R. (2002). *Usability inspections by groups of specialists: Perceived agreement in spite of disparate observations* (pp. 662–663). Extended abstracts on human factors in computing systems (*CHI EA'02*). New York, NY: ACM Press.

Hornbæk, K., & Frøkjaer, E. (2005). *Comparing usability problems and redesign proposal as input to practical systems development* (pp. 391–400). In: *Proceedings of the SIGCHI conference on human factors in computing systems (CHI'05).* New York, NY: ACM.

Hwang, W., & Salvendy, G. (2010). Number of people required for usability evaluation: The 10 ± 2 rule. *Communications of the ACM, 53*(5), 130–133.

IEEE Std 1028-2008 (2008). *IEEE standard for software reviews. IEEE standards software engineering.* New York, NY: The Institute of Electrical and Electronics Engineering.

Jacobsen, N. E., Hertzum, M., & John, B. E. (1998a). The evaluator effect in usability studies: Problem detection and severity judgments. In: *Proceedings of the Human Factors and Ergonomics Society*1336–1340.

Jacobsen, N. E., Hertzum, M., & John, B. E. (1998b). *The evaluator effect in usability tests* (pp. 255–256). CHI'98 conference summary on human factors in computing systems *(CHI'98)*. New York, NY: ACM.

Jaferian, P., Hawkey, K., Sotirakopoulos, A., Velez-Rojas, M., & Beznosov, K. (2011). Heuristics for evaluating IT security management tools (Article 7, 20 pages). In: *Proceedings of the seventh symposium on usable privacy and security (SOUPS'11)*. New York, NY: ACM.

Jeffries, R., Miller, J. R., Wharton, C., & Uyeda, K. M. (1991). User interface evaluation in the real world: A comparison of four techniques. In: *Proceedings from ACM CHI'91 conference* (pp. 119–124). New Orleans, LA, April 28–May 2, 1991.

John, B. E., & Packer, H. (1995). Learning and using the cognitive walkthrough method: A case study approach. In: *Proceedings of CHI'95* (pp. 429–436). Denver, CO, May 1995. New York, NY: ACM Press.

Kahn, M. K., & Prail, A. (1994). Formal usability inspections. In J. Nielsen, & R. L. Mack (Eds.), *Usability inspection methods* (pp. 141–171). New York, NY: John Wiley & Sons.

Kantner, L., Shroyer, R., & Rosenbaum, S. (2002). Structured heuristic evaluation of online documentation. In: *Proceedings of IEEE international professional communication conference (IPCC 2002)* (Portland, OR, USA, September 17–20, 2002).

Karoulis, A., & Pombortsis, A. S. (2004). Heuristic evaluation of web-sites: The evaluators' expertise and the appropriate criteria list. *Informatics in Education, 3*(2), 55–74.

Kirmani, S., & Rajasekarn, S. (2007). Heuristic evaluation quality score (HEQS): A measure of heuristic evaluation skills. *Journal of Usability Studies, 2*(2), 61–75.

Kotval, X. P., Coyle, C. L., Santos, P. A., Vaughn, H., & Iden, R. (2007). *Heuristic evaluations at Bell labs: Analyses of evaluator overlap and group session* (pp. 1729–1734). Extended Abstracts on Human Factors in Computing Systems *(CHI EA'07)*. New York, NY: ACM Press.

Krug, S. (2009). *Rocket surgery made easy: The do-it-yourself guide to finding and fixing usability problems*. Berkeley, CA: New Riders.

Kurosu, M., Matsuura, S., Sugizaki, M. (1997). Categorical inspection method—structured heuristic evaluation (sHEM). In: *IEEE International Conference on Systems, Man, and Cybernetics* (pp. 2613–2618). Piscataway, NJ: IEEE.

Laitenberger, O., & Atkinson, C. (1999). *Generalizing perspective-based inspection to handle object-oriented development artifacts* (pp. 494–503). In: *Proceedings of the 21st international conference on software engineering (ICSE'99)*. New York, NY: ACM.

Lauesen, S. (2005). *User interface design: A software engineering perspective*. Harlow, England: Addison-Wesley.

Lewis, C., Polson, P., Wharton, C., & Rieman, J. (1990). Testing a walkthrough methodology for theory-based design of walk-up-and-use interfaces. In J. Carrasco, & J. Whiteside (Eds.), *Proceedings of ACM CHI'90: Conference on human factors in computer systems* (pp. 235–242). New York, NY: ACM Press.

Lewis, C., & Wharton, C. (1997). Cognitive walkthroughs. In M. Helander, T. K. Landauer, & P. Prabhu (Eds.), *Handbook of human-computer interaction* (2nd ed., pp. 717–732). Amsterdam, the Netherlands: Elsevier Science.

Linderman, M., & Fried, J. (2004). *Defensive design for the web: How to improve error messages, help, forms, and other crisis points*. Berkeley, CA: New Riders.

Mahatody, T., Sagar, M., & Kolski, C. (2010). State of the art on the cognitive walkthrough method, its variants and evolutions. *International Journal of Human Computer Interaction, 26*(8), 741–785.

Mankoff, J., Dey, A. K., Hsieh, G., Kientz, J., Lederer, S., & Ames, M. (2003). *Heuristic evaluation of ambient displays* (pp. 169–176). In: *Proceedings of the SIGCHI conference on human factors in computing systems (CHI'03)*. New York, NY: ACM.

Markopoulos, P., Read, J. C., MacFarlane, S., & Hoysniemi, J. (2008). *Evaluating children's interactive products: Principles and practices for interaction designers*. Burlington, MA: Morgan Kaufmann.

Molich, R. (2011). *Comparative usability evaluation reports.* Retrieved August 10, 2013, from <http://www.dialogdesign.dk/CUE-9.htm>

Molich, R. (2013). *Usability testing myths.* Retrieved July 25, 2013, from <http://www.netmagazine.com/features/usability-testing-myths>

Molich, R., & Dumas, J. S. (2008). Comparative usability evaluation (CUE-4). *Behaviour and Information Technology, 27*, 3.

Monk, A., Wright, P., Haber, J., & Davenport, L. (1993). *Improving your human-computer interface: A practical technique*. Prentice Hall International (UK) Ltd.

Muller, M. J., Matheson, L., Page, C., & Gallup, R. (1998). Methods & tools: Participatory heuristic evaluation. *Interactions, 5*(5), 13.

Nielesen, J., & Tahir, M. (2002). *Homepage usability: 50 websites deconstructed*. Berkeley, CA: New Riders.

Nielsen, J. (1992). Finding usability problems through heuristic evaluation. In P. Bauersfeld, J. Bennett, & G. Lynch (Eds.), *Proceedings of the SIGCHI conference on human factors in computing systems (CHI'92)* (pp. 373–380). New York, NY: ACM Press.

Nielsen, J. (1993). *Usability engineering*. San Francisco, CA: Morgan Kaufmann.

Nielsen, J. (1994a). Heuristic evaluation. In J. Nielsen, & R. L. Mack (Eds.), *Usability inspection methods*. New York, NY: Wiley.

Nielsen, J. (1994b). Enhancing the explanatory power of usability heuristics. In B. Adelson, S. Dumais, & J. Olson (Eds.), *Proceedings of the SIGCHI conference on human factors in computing systems (CHI'94)* (pp. 152–158). New York, NY: ACM Press.

Nielsen, J., & Mack, R. (Eds.), (1994). *Usability inspection methods* New York, NY: Wiley.

Nielsen, J., & Molich, R. (1990). Heuristic evaluation of user interfaces. In J. Carrasco Chew, & J. Whiteside (Eds.), *Proceedings of the SIGCHI conference on human factors in computing systems (CHI'90)* (pp. 249–256). New York, NY: ACM Press.

Novick, D. G. (1999). Using the cognitive walkthrough for operating procedures. *Interactions, 6*(3), 31–37.

Polson, P., & Lewis, C. H. (1990). *Theory-based design for easily learned interfaces, Human-computer interaction* (Vol. 5, pp. 191–220). Hillsdale, NJ: Lawrence Erlbaum Associates.

Pruitt, J., & Adlin, T. (2005). *The persona lifecycle: Keeping people in mind throughout product design*. San Francisco, CA: Morgan Kaufmann Publishers.

Purho, V. (2000). *Heuristic inspections for documentation: 10 recommended documentation heuristics.* Retrieved August 1, 2013, from <http://www.stcsig.org/usability/newsletter/0004-docsheuristics.html>

Rosenbaum, S., Rohn, J., & Humberg, J. (2000). *A toolkit for strategic usability: Results from workshops, panels, and surveys* (pp. 337–344). In: *Proceedings of CHI 2000*. New York, NY: ACM Press.

Rowley, D. E., & Rhoades, D. G. (1992). *The cognitive jogthrough: A fast-paced user interface evaluation procedure* (pp. 389–395). In: *Proceedings of ACM CHI'92 conference on human factors in computing systems*. New York, NY: ACM Press.

Sawyer, P., Flanders, A., & Wixon, D. (1996). Making a difference—the impact of inspections. In M. J. Tauber (Ed.), *Proceedings of the SIGCHI conference on human factors in computing systems (CHI'96)* (pp. 376–382). New York, NY: ACM.

Schrage, M. (2000). *Serious play: How the world's best companies simulate to innovate.* Boston, MA: Harvard Business School Press.

Sears, A. (1997). Heuristic walkthroughs. Finding the problems without the noise. *International Journal of Human-Computer Interaction, 9*(3), 213–234.

Sears, A., & Hess, D. J. (1998). *The effect of task description detail on evaluator performance with cognitive walkthroughs* (pp. 259–260). In: *Proceedings of ACM CHI'98: Conference on human factors in computing systems.* New York, NY: ACM Press.

Shneiderman, B. (1987). *Designing the user interface: Strategies for effective human-computer interaction.* Reading, MA: Addison-Wesley.

Shneiderman, B., & Plaisant, C. (2010). *Designing the user interface: Strategies for effective human-computer interaction* (5th ed.). Boston, MA: Addison-Wesley.

Shull, F., Rus, I., & Basili, V. (2000). How perspective-based reading can improve requirements inspections. *IEEE Computer, 33*(7), 73–79.

Slavkovic, A., & Cross, K. (1999). *Novice heuristic evaluations of a complex interface* (pp. 304–305). CHI'99 extended abstracts on human factors in computing systems *(CHI EA'99)*. New York, NY: ACM.

Spencer, R. (2000). *The streamlined cognitive walkthrough method, working around social constraints encountered in a software development company* (pp. 353–359). In: *Proceedings of the SIGCHI: Conference on human factors in computing systems (CHI'00).* New York, NY: ACM Press.

Stacy, W., & MacMillan, J. (1995). Cognitive bias in software engineering. *Communications of the ACM, 38*(6), 57–63.

Stone, D., Jarrett, C., Woodroffe, M., & Minocha, S. (2005). *User interface design and evaluation.* San Francisco, CA: Morgan Kaufmann.

Tsui, K. M., Abu-Zahra, K., Casipe, R., M'Sadoques, J., & Drury, J. L. (2010). *Developing heuristics for assistive robotics* (pp. 193–194). In: *Proceedings of the fifth ACM/IEEE international conference on Human-robot interaction (HRI'10).* Piscataway, NJ: IEEE Press.

Usability Body of Knowledge. (n.d.). Pluralistic usability walkthrough. Retrieved October 29, 2013 from < http://www.usabilitybok.org/pluralistic-walkthrough >.

Usability First Glossary. (n.d.). Retrieved June 14, 2004, from <http://www.usabilityfirst.com/glossary/term_306.txl>

Virzi, R. (1997). Usability inspection methods. In M. G. Helander, T. K. Landauer, & P. V. Prabhu (Eds.), *Handbook of human-computer interaction* (2nd ed.). Englewood Cliffs, NJ: Elsevier Science.

Weinschenk, S., & Barker, D. (2000). *Designing effective speech interfaces.* New York, NY: Wiley.

Wharton, C., Bradford, J., Jeffries, J., & Franzke, M. (1992). Applying cognitive walkthroughs to more complex user interfaces: Experiences, issues and recommendations. In P. Bauersfeld, J. Bennett, & G. Lynch (Eds.), *Proceedings of the SIGCHI conference on human factors in computing systems (CHI'92)* (pp. 381–388). New York, NY: ACM.

Wharton, C., Rieman, J., Lewis, C., & Polson, P. (1994). The cognitive walkthrough: A practitioner's guide. In J. Nielsen, & R. L. Mack (Eds.), *Usability inspections methods* (pp. 105–140). New York, NY: Wiley.

Wiegers, K. E. (2002). *Peer reviews in software: A practical guide.* Boston, MA: Addison-Wesley.

Wilson, C. (2009). *The consistency conundrum.* Retrieved July 26, 2013, from <http://dux.typepad.com/dux/2009/03/the-consistency-conundrum.html>

Wilson, C. (2011). *Perspective-based inspection.* Retrieved July 26, 2013, from <http://dux.typepad.com/dux/2011/03/method-10-of-100-perspective-based-inspection.html>

Wilson, C. E. (2006). Triangulation: The explicit use of multiple methods, measures, and approaches for determining core issues in product development. *Interactions, 13*(6), 46-ff.

Wilson, C. E. (2007). The problem with usability problems: Context is critical. *Interactions, 14*(5), 46-ff.

Wixon, D., & Wilson, C. E. (1998). *The usability engineering framework for product design and evaluation Handbook of human-computer interaction* (2nd ed., pp. 653–688). Amsterdam, the Netherlands: Elsevier.

Yehuda, H., & McGinn, J. (2007). *Coming to terms: Comparing and combining the results of multiple evaluators performing heuristic evaluation* (pp. 1899–1904). *CHI'07: Extended abstracts on human factors in computing systems.* New York, NY: ACM Press.

Zhang, Z., Basili, V., & Shneiderman, B. (1999). Perspective-based usability inspection: An empirical validation of efficiency. *Empirical Software Engineering, 4*(1), 43–69.

Printed and bound by CPI Group (UK) Ltd, Croydon, CR0 4YY

03/10/2024

01040423-0013